MW00851029

100-Word Stories is a revelation. Culbertson and Faulkner's helpful book offers the perfect platform for students to learn and practice the essential skills of writing. It also helps them be more critical readers as it shows them how to explore the myriad decisions writers make to express and convey ideas. It offers teachers profound insights into writing instruction and provides deep understanding of the writing process. Filled with examples and thoughtful reflection questions, their practical and classroom-friendly guidance provides a clear pathway to helping students to unlock the stories hiding within them.

–Peter Brunn, author of *The Lesson Planning Handbook*

Teachers of writing and literature—as well as practicing writers—love 100-word stories, and this book is exactly the resource teachers need to bring those little gems into their classrooms. Culbertson and Faulkner, themselves masters of the craft, show us how 100-word stories are not only short but also impeccably crafted, revealing so much in such a concentrated form. In addition to practical advice, the book includes a wealth of 100-word stories suitable for classrooms from fifth grade through high school.

**–Elyse Eidman-Aadahl, Executive Director,
National Writing Project**

100-WORD
STORIES

To Kathy,

Write big! Write small!
Just write!

Big thanks!
Grant Faulkner
9/23/24

100-WORD STORIES

A SHORT FORM FOR EXPANSIVE WRITING

KIM CULBERTSON

with Grant Faulkner

HEINEMANN • Portsmouth, NH

Heinemann
145 Maplewood Avenue, Suite 300
Portsmouth, NH 03801
www.heinemann.com

© 2024 by Kim Culbertson and Grant Faulkner

All rights reserved, including but not limited to the right to reproduce this book, or portions thereof, in any form or by any means whatsoever, without written permission from the publisher. For information on permission for reproductions or subsidiary rights licensing, please contact Heinemann at permissions@heinemann.com.

Heinemann's authors have devoted their entire careers to developing the unique content in their works, and their written expression is protected by copyright law. We respectfully ask that you do not adapt, reuse, or copy anything on third-party (whether for-profit or not-for-profit) lesson-sharing websites.

—Heinemann Publishers

"Dedicated to Teachers" is a trademark of Greenwood Publishing Group, LLC.

The authors and publisher wish to thank those who have generously given permission to reprint borrowed material:

Page 5: Faulkner, Grant. "Shirley Temple." Copyright Grant Faulkner. Reprinted with permission.
Pages 13–14: Zentner, Jeffrey Dean. "The Spot." Copyright Jeffrey Dean Zentner. Reprinted with permission.
Page 18: Campbell, Tara. "The Greatest Show." Copyright Tara Campbell. Reprinted with permission.
Page 23: Valin, Julie. "Leaving It." Copyright Julie Valin. Reprinted with permission.

Acknowledgments for borrowed material continue on page viii.

Library of Congress Control Number: 2023914335
ISBN: 978-0-325-13720-9

Acquisitions Editor: Zoë Ryder White
Production Editor: Victoria Merecki
Cover and Interior Designer: Suzanne Heiser
Typesetter: Shawn Girsberger
Manufacturing: Jaime Spaulding

Printed in the United States of America on acid-free paper

1 2 3 4 5 VP 27 26 25 24 23 PO 4500797720

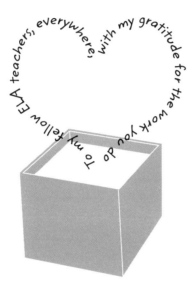

To my fellow ELA teachers, everywhere, with my gratitude for the work you do

Credits continued from copyright page

Page 28–29: Lawrence, Tabitha. "Desert, Spring." Copyright Tabitha Lawrence. Reprinted with permission.

Page 33: Lee, Stacey. "Daddy's Flask." Copyright Stacey Lee. Reprinted with permission.

Page 45: Hsu Gee, Darien. "Sous." Copyright Darien Hsu Gee. Reprinted with permission.

Page 48: Casey, Kirsten. "Power Outage." Copyright Kirsten Casey. Reprinted with permission.

Page 49: Casey, Kirsten. "Tonight." Copyright Kirsten Casey. Reprinted with permission.

Page 55: West, Kasie. "Fences." Copyright Kasie West. Reprinted with permission.

Pages 58–59: Taylor, Jessica. "Places that Know You." Copyright Jessica Taylor. Reprinted with permission.

Page 62: Rutten, Amy. "Under the Rainbow." Copyright Amy Rutten. Reprinted with permission.

Page 70: Walker, Ran. "Rainbow." Copyright Randolph Walker, Jr. Reprinted with permission.

Pages 73–74: Woods, Darcy. "More Than a Waitress." Copyright Darcy Woods. Reprinted with permission.

Page 91: McNeil, Gretchen. "Mirror, Mirror." Copyright Gretchen McNeil. Reprinted with permission.

Pages 102–03, 104: Teferet, Rachel. "Bantam Chicken." Copyright Rachel Rosen-Carroll. Reprinted with permission.

Page 107: Culbertson, Kim. "Band Shed." Copyright Kim Culbertson. Reprinted with permission.

Page 108: Culbertson, Kim. "Spoon Trouble." Copyright Kim Culbertson. Reprinted with permission.

Page 109: Culbertson, Kim. "Ready." Copyright Kim Culbertson. Reprinted with permission.

Page 110: Culbertson, Kim. "Dead Tired." Copyright Kim Culbertson. Reprinted with permission.

Page 117: Dwyer, Kristin. "The Ticket." Copyright Kristin Dwyer. Reprinted with permission.

Page 118: Sugiura, Misa. "Quitter." Copyright Misa Sugiura. Reprinted with permission.

Page 126: Culbertson, Kim. "Jack-O'-Lantern." Copyright Kim Culbertson. Reprinted with permission.

Page 127: Hall, Sands. "Setting the Table." Copyright Sands Hall. Reprinted with permission.

Pages 127–28: Wright, Gary. "The Believer." Copyright Gary Wright. Reprinted with permission.

Image Credits

Rope bow: Essl/Shutterstock.com

Gift box: phive/Shutterstock.com

Water splash: HardtIllustrations/Shutterstock.com

Figure 22.1: © Joyseulay/Shutterstock/HIP

Author photo for Kim Culbertson: © Josh Miller Photography

Author photo for Grant Faulkner: © Dan Cowles

Mad Men® is a registered trademark of Lions Gate Entertainment Inc. Skittles® is a registered trademark of Wm. Wrigley Jr. Company. Chevron® is a registered trademark of Chevron Intellectual Property LLC. Coke® is a registered trademark of The Coca-Cola Company. Save Mart® is a registered trademark of Save Mart Supermarkets LLC. Mustang® is a registered trademark of Ford Motor Company. Cheetos® is a registered trademark of Frito-Lay North America, Inc. Instagram® and the Camera logos are trademarks of Instagram, LLC in the United States and elsewhere. Mercedes-Benz® is a registered trademark of Daimler AG. Reese's Book Club® is a registered trademark of Be Sunshine, LLC. David Bowie® is a registered trademark of Jones-Tintoretto Entertainment Company LLC. The Beatles® is a registered trademark of Apple Corps Limited. Marvel® is a registered trademark of of The Walt Disney Company. Lord of the Rings® is a registered trademark of Middle-earth Enterprises. Google™ is a trademark of Google LLC. Waterstones® is a registered trademark of Waterstones Booksellers Limited. Pringles® is a registered trademark of The Proctor and Gamble Company. Band-Aid® is a registered trademark of Johnson & Johnson. Netflix® is a registered trademark of Netflix, Inc. The Witcher® is a registered trademark of CD PROJEKT S.A. Bridgerton® is a registered trademark of Netflix Studios, LLC. BuzzFeed® is a registered trademark of BuzzFeed, Inc. Zoom® is a registered trademark of Zoom Video Communications, Inc.

Contents

Online Resources

Some of the discussion questions and writing exercises associated with the 100-word stories suggest that students have their own copies to annotate, so we've added each of the stories, chapter by chapter, to the online resources as downloadable files. For access to the stories and several other student resources:

1. Go to **http://hein.pub/100Words-login**.

2. Log in with your username and password. If you do not already have an account with Heinemann, you will need to create an account.

3. On the Welcome page, choose "**Click here to register an Online Resource.**"

4. Register your product by entering the code **SHORTFORM** (be sure to read and check the acknowledgment box under the keycode).

5. Once you have registered your product, it will appear alphabetically in your account list under "**My Online Resources.**"

Note: When returning to Heinemann.com to access your previously registered products, simply log in to your Heinemann account and click on "**View my registered Online Resources.**"

Part One: Foundational Elements

Part Two: Elements of Language

Acknowledgments

This book wouldn't be here without the encouragement of Grant Faulkner and Elyse Eidman-Aadahl. Thank you both for believing in these small, bright stories and in my ability to share them with other teachers and writers.

Thank you to my students who first told me how much fun they were having with these stories and then wrote some for me. And thank you to all the teen and professional writers who answered the call to write a piece for this book. Your work will brighten so many classrooms.

I am especially thankful to Kirsten Casey and Beret Olsen for your guidance with the student authors. There was so much teaching done before this book even saw the light of day. You two do such beautiful work in the world.

Thank you to Zoë Ryder White for plucking my proposal from the pile, seeing its potential, and encouraging me step-by-step as this book found its way. You are the brightest of editors. And I'm grateful to Heinemann for giving this book its home. I know what good hands it's in. I want to specifically thank Michelle Flynn, Tessa Hathaway, and Victoria Merecki.

I am so grateful to my professional school communities both at Forest Charter School and Dominican University of California. One thing I've learned after twenty-five years in education is that you need your people to survive. This work can be exhausting, immersive, beautiful, and frustrating, but it is made more meaningful knowing other people care about it just as much as I do.

Finally, I want to thank my husband, Peter Sagebiel, also a veteran educator, for his love for and encouragement of this book. Also, my daughter, Ana, who is studying education in college no matter how much we warn her off ;) You wonderful bright thing, you.

Introduction

From Grant

I had an epiphany one day while I was volunteering in my daughter's second-grade class during a writing lesson. I observed as the teacher guided the students to flesh out their stories beyond the short, blunt sentences most of them had written and to capture the world more vividly with more detail, more feeling, more words. She was doing her job, and doing it well—making the world come alive through language—but I began to think of the role that "more" plays in most writers' development.

I remembered how when I was assigned a paper when I was in high school, our first question was always, "How long does it have to be?" And then we wrote in order to reach that page count, padding the paper with extra research or extra words, especially those of us who knew that a good way to get an A was to write longer papers with big words we found in the thesaurus.

This is all good in those early stages of writing. We need to try on those big words. We need to be ambitious with language to explore the bigness of our thoughts and learn how to fill pages and push boundaries. But that bigness also needs a counterpoint, a question. We need to recognize the different ways that smallness can work to open up an idea, how less is often the best way to reveal a dramatic moment.

We live in a culture that celebrates bigness—big houses, big vehicles, big meals—so bigness is generally valued more than smallness in most matters. In fact, even though length was not mentioned in the SAT essay grading rubric back when the essay was part of the SAT, a study revealed that the longer an essay was, the higher the score tended to be.

The length of papers increases with each grade level, and students' writing lives essentially become apprenticeships with "more" as they bulk up their texts, using bigger and more jargonistic language as they proceed through college and graduate school. It's as if writers are taught to prove their smarts by flexing their writerly muscles, pumping up their prose with multisyllabic curlicues and complex structures.

Good writing, however, is so often about less. It's about succinctness and clarity. It's about evocation and mood. It's about suspense and omission. It's about finding the right word, not more words.

I learned all those elements later in my writing life, after years of trying to write novels with an ever-expansive aesthetic of what I call "maximalist comprehensiveness," full of crisscrossing tentacles of storylines and sentences stuffed with syntactic flourishes. But then I discovered 100-word stories one day by chance, and I became addicted to writing these mysterious little stories because of the way I had to move a story not by including more, but by telling less. I had to find the essence of a story, not its sprawl. I had to learn how to tell a story through a simple detail, a hint, instead of the layers of a backstory. I had to work with the gaps of text rather than stuffing things in to fill the gaps.

It was a different kind of writing and reading. Most of my writing life had been a training ground of "more," so I'd never been taught to write less, to focus on what could be removed from a story or an essay rather than what could be added. I'd never thought about how "bigness" can reside in tiny things, how stories can reside on the borders of a poem, opening up to include the reader as if the reader is a co-writer of the story.

I'm often asked if one can tell a story in just 100 words. As *100-Word Stories* shows, the answer is yes. Kim Culbertson has written a brilliant guide based on her classroom experiences of teaching 100-word stories. She explores all the traditional elements of writing a story—setting, plot, character, conflict, imagery, theme—and, in fact, because these stories are so short, those elements become more noticeable—brighter, even—so students can focus on them more precisely.

"It might seem almost impossible to enclose the great movement of the universe in such a narrow space. But through a kind of magic, the poet manages to make the infinite enter into that small cell. There, every surprise may fit," wrote Jorge Carrera Andrade (2011).

These stories might be small cells, but they teem with life when looked at under a microscope. May *100-Word Stories* be that microscope for you and your students. I know you'll see things about stories and writing that might previously have been invisible. I know your writing and reading will never quite be the same when you experience the infinite that swirls about in these small cells.

From Kim

Small, Bright Things

It's likely that most ELA teachers have been in the situation I found myself in one day: asking a question about a longer piece of writing our class was reading, and getting . . . crickets. I cleared my throat and tried to rephrase, hoping to get someone to say *something* about the piece. Nothing. Zip. Nada.

Next class, I changed gears. I loaded a 100-word story onto Google Classroom, read it to them, and had them read it again. Right then. On the spot. Then I asked the same questions I'd asked before: "What's important about where this is set? Who are these characters? What do they want? What are the themes?"

Hands went up. More than several. What was happening?

I kept bringing in stories. They kept responding. So I had them write some, centering on a list of themes we'd generated from the stories we'd been reading. They wrote for me. And wrote. And wrote.

I started referring to these stories as "Small, Bright Things" because they brought with them a sort of magic to my classroom. They glimmered, breathing new life into our study of literature and our original writing.

When I first started assigning 100-word stories, one of my students said in surprise, "It's like all the parts of a real story, but short!" I love this—even as I explained to her that a 100-word story is a *real* story, she was spot on about its parts. This is the beauty of using these stories to teach exploration and analysis of individual literary elements. In another class, we were unpacking a student's original 100-word story when one of his classmates pointed out to him, "You devote sixty-two words to setting—that leaves almost nothing for all the other stuff!"

All that other stuff is what this teaching guide breaks down. All the parts—not just of a short story, but of any longer piece of fiction too: character, setting, point of view, conflict/tension, sensory description, arc, theme. Each 100-word story allows students to explore a structure that holds all these essential literary elements in an easily digestible package. I have found that working with this form before we dig into larger pieces, or during the study of longer pieces, enables my students to more readily recognize these elements in any piece of literature, because the study of these 100-word stories teaches them to identify a story's intrinsic architecture.

When studying stories with my students, I generally group fiction elements into three categories: **foundational**, **language-based**, and **structural**.

Foundational elements are any element a story simply can't exist without: POV, setting, plot, character, conflict/tension, etc.

Elements of **language** are sentence-specific: sensory language, imagery, active language, symbolism, etc.

Structural elements, for me, are things like form/structure, theme, genre, dialogue, arc (the way an author tracks plot across a story), subtext/backstory, etc.

As a fiction writer, I understand that any of these elements could be grouped differently, but this is one way to look at the architecture of a story, the specific choices/tools a writer uses to build a story, and their purposes within the storytelling. For the sake of this book, I grouped them this way, but you should feel free to move them wherever makes sense for your classroom.

I have divided this book into four sections and twenty-five chapters. You can use it comprehensively or jump around based on your needs. I've included in each chapter discussion questions that you can assign for written response or use for class discussion. I've designed the writing exercises to be done in class, but these can obviously also be homework assignments. The exercises are less formal—they are meant to be generative and to get those creative ideas flowing. I've centered the writing practice around the development of a 100-word story portfolio for your students to develop throughout the year. But again—mix it up, use one thing or all the things. I just hope you find something that lights up your classroom the way these small, bright things have lit up mine.

Content Disclaimer

It is no easy task to design a book meant for fifth- through twelfth-grade classroom use, and as a result not every story in the book will be appropriate for every grade level (not to mention, different people have different levels of comfort when it comes to content). We tried to include at least one story in each section that could work for each concept at any grade level, five through twelve.

a writer is always "noticing"—noticing the way people interact with each other, the way they speak. This noticing (and the specific choices we make in response to it) allows us to create unique, vibrant worlds in small spaces, and these worlds begin at the sentence level. Below, see the homework assignment I give my students. I share it with them as an online document you could download it from the online resources. Over the years, many teachers have talked to me about this assignment. As Grant Faulkner wrote in *Pep Talks for Writers*, "much of writing is about 'seeing'—about noticing the specific senses that allow us to experience the world—sight, smell, taste, touch, sound. For this assignment, they can be just words and phrases—and spend approximately thirty minutes noticing everything about what you see, smell, taste, touch, and hear, jot down notes about what you discover in that place, but also try to record the unique, specific details in sensory detail. The reason I refer to these 100-word stories as "small" is its attention to detail, the precise introduction to this form is its attention to detail, the introduction to this vignette; they don't have to be complete sentences or a full story; to try to record the unique, vibrant worlds in their worlds. Because of it allows us to create unique, beautiful and interesting and heartbreaking. The magic of the form is its attention to detail, a story, not its sprawl. I had to tell a story through a particular word rather than stuffing things in to fill the gaps." And we are noticing the specific sensory details instead of the layers of a backstory. A writer must do so much because each one must do so much.

PART ONE

FOUNDATIONAL ELEMENTS

What the Story Can't Live Without

I define foundational elements for my students as the pieces a story can't live without. I tell them that these foundational elements are fairly straightforward: a story is told through a specific lens (point of view, referred to throughout as POV) about a character who lives in an environment, who is experiencing a moment of change, and for whom something is "at stake." Every story has these elements. There are many other elements I will get to later, but I always have my students start here: POV, character, setting, conflict.

1

POINT OF VIEW (POV)

Featured Authors: Cole Gibson, age 12, and Grant Faulkner

My students are likely tired of hearing me say, "Point of view is everything," but the more I write and study story, the more I think it must be. I could write an entire book exploring the role of POV in a piece of fiction. It's a complex concept. But this is not that book, so we'll keep to the basics.

Simply put, POV is the lens through which the story is being told.

For me as a writer and reader, the essential thing to know is this lens is the cornerstone of the way an author tells the story. It is the place where the narrator stands. Sometimes that is first person, sometimes it is third-person close or distant, and sometimes it is omniscient. Therefore, because of this *purposeful* lens, the point of view of a story determines the information we receive as readers.

An author chooses a point of view by deciding whether the story is set from a first-person or third-person perspective or from an omniscient point of view. Authors also choose to set the story in the past tense or the present tense. Each of these decisions shapes the lens of the story. Therefore, what we as readers know about the point of view allows us to understand our relationship to the storytelling. Will we be getting one person's perspective the entire time (first person and third-person limited) or will we be getting more of a bird's-eye view with an all-knowing narrator (omniscient)? Will the story be told through only one lens? Or will there be multiple lenses? Is the story more reflective (past tense) or immediate (present tense)?

Like I said, it's complex.

POV has its own attitude, voice, and position. POV determines the way everything in the story gets shaped (the verbs and adjectives, the character attributes, the specific images all exist as ways of revealing this lens). If a narrator is a dancer, the story must be told through the eyes of this particular dancer's experiences. If the narrator is a tiger, the story can only describe things a tiger would know or see. Once, when I was workshopping my first novel, *Songs for a Teenage Nomad*, someone asked me about a specific line, "Is this Calle here or *you*, as the author?" It was an essential question for me to think about as the author. It had to be Calle, my first-person POV; it couldn't be *me*, Kim. I wasn't telling the story—Calle was.

POV gives us clues about the story. It can often be the starting point for discussing everything else: setting, character, conflict, etc. An author chooses words on purpose. These words build the sentences that build the paragraphs that ultimately build the entire story—all funneled through a specific POV.

In Cole Gibson's story that follows, the POV is first person, a young person taking a family trip. Notice right away that this narrator opens with "after an eternity" while the parents give directions. The use of "eternity" shows us instantly that this narrator, this POV, feels like this trip is taking forever. It positions us in this specific point of view, with its mood, attitude, and lens.

Let's read Cole's story "Silence" and investigate his choices.

Silence

We're here. After an eternity of Mom and Dad saying, "Turn left here, James!" and "I know, Sharon!" Finally. Muir Woods National Monument. We park, and I immediately sprint toward the entrance, leaving the bickering behind. There they are, standing tall and proud. Redwoods. After twenty minutes of Mom and Dad yelling about which trail is shortest, we choose one. I smell the fresh air and look up at the sun peering through the trees onto the ground. I could stay in this moment forever. For a minute, Mom and Dad stop fighting, look up at the trees, and smile.

—COLE GIBSON

DISCUSSION

After your students read "Silence," have them underline two places in the story that demonstrate the point of view, and then discuss:

1. Who is telling this story?
2. How does the first-person perspective shape our understanding of the story?
3. In what tense is this story told?
4. How does this tense make it more immediate?

Writing Exercise

Ask your students to choose three lines from the story and write them in third person, past tense instead of first person, present. How does this shift to a different POV change the story? How does it stay the same?

Tense is essential to knowing where a narrator is seated, but sometimes an author can surprise us with a tense change. See if you can spot the tense change in Grant Faulkner's story, "Shirley Temple."

Shirley Temple

I sat at the bar, my feet swinging from a stool. Jacksonville, 1972. The adults crowded into a circular booth in the corner. Men pinched women. Women squirmed in squirmy dresses. I smelled the chlorine on my hands as I listened to the cackles of laughter. My father told me I could have as many Shirley Temples as I wanted, but I drank slowly, counting to fifty before taking a single bird-like sip. The cherry bobbed slowly lower in the glass, almost dissolving like candy. I wouldn't eat it until it rested on the bottom. It's good to have rules.

—GRANT FAULKNER

DISCUSSION

1. Where does this story change tense?
2. How does this tense change shift the story for us or give us greater insight?
3. What might be a reason Grant did this?

Once you've discussed these questions with your students, have them read about (or read to them) Grant's choices in his own words.

I once heard the creator of the TV show Mad Men®, *Matt Weiner, speak, and he said he envisioned the show as if he was looking through a keyhole into his parents' lives. That's how I thought of the boy in my story, "Shirley Temple." He's an unwanted companion in this scene of adult decadence, so his father sticks him at the bar and essentially has the bartender be his babysitter.*

Because he is abandoned, not a part of things, yet still present, the boy becomes a witness. This is the place I like to reside most in a story (and in life). While we don't get many details into what happens between the men and the women he watches, we get enough to know that people are doing things they shouldn't, and, like the boy, we can imagine the things that might happen offscreen.

I could have written this in the point of view of third-person omniscience, but I would have lost that touch of poignancy and vulnerability that's created by seeing the scene through the boy's eyes. The story is about what he feels about being in the presence of his father's misbehavior, and the reader needs to feel the character change that happens, the moral stance of restraint he takes by not allowing himself to drink as many Shirley Temples as he wants. Third-person omniscience would have provided more distance, another layer of witnessing, and taken the reader a step further away from the drama.

It's amazing what you can see just by looking through a tiny keyhole. Or from a barstool.

Writing Practice

Have students write a 100-word story with a purposeful POV choice (present, past, or a switch!). Encourage them to set this story somewhere interesting that allows the character to feel or learn something during the journey.

Story Portfolio

If you'll be using this book either as a complete unit or through-out the year with your students in a deep way (or even just once in a while), it helps to have the students keep a portfolio of their stories (either virtually or in a paper format) so they can see all their stories in one place and have them in one place for the revision portion of this book.

TIE-IN TO CLASSROOM READING

Look at a passage (the opening always works well) of the novel or story that you're reading as a class and explore the POV choice. Have students write about any specifics they notice that demonstrate the POV.

2

CHARACTER

Featured Authors: Bryce Kemble, age 16, and Luella Dang, age 16

REVIEW TERM: POV

Characters drive a story. What they want. What obstacles are in their way. What kind of personalities they have and how these personalities move them through whatever world they are in. The most important thing when writing a character should be creating specificity. Writers use specific detail to create a unique individual and they can show this uniqueness in a variety of ways.

In Bryce Kemble's story "Sight of Sound" the character has a condition called "synesthesia," in which more than one of someone's senses are stimulated rather than just one sense. For example, in Bryce's story the character "sees" sound.

Sight of Sound

He sees sound. When he hears something, psychedelic images form colorful dust. But he's anxious his art copies other art, probably because he's been told his paintings look like something seen before. He tries to be indifferent, but he struggles to find direction, joyless.

One Saturday, he leaves his bungalow, hearing the roar of the nearby train. Blinking, he witnesses patterns that grow stronger as the train draws close. He closes his eyes, filled with awe. Space, with orange and blue dust in motion, circulates and clashes. He hurries inside, begins setting things up.

Everything silent, he paints from memory.

—BRYCE KEMBLE

A character's specificity can also feel universal. They might experience something many readers have experienced, and this creates a meaningful, relatable connection with the reader. For example, in Luella Dang's story "Walls" her character is going through the process of saying goodbye to childhood friends this narrator no longer feels connected with. Luella blends the specific images of this character's bedroom wall photos with the universal feeling of moving on.

Walls

The pieces of paper, art, and memorabilia that live on my walls know they have a short lifetime, will soon be reincarnated.

As my midwestern life changes, so do my walls. The walls plastered with colors stand before me, new poster in hand. I brought home some school spirit after viewing colleges in Oregon.

I study a photo collage of some smiling childhood friends as I decide where to place my poster. I haven't been close to these smiles in years. If I took all the photos down, I'd have a perfect spot for my poster.

I take them down.

—LUELLA DANG

Ultimately, it's important to emphasize that authors can define characters in multiple ways. It's easy to think of a character in terms of appearance, but there is so much more to a person than physical attributes. Think of a character in terms of something specific—whether that is a skill, an interior attribute (like self-awareness), or an emotive attribute (like friendliness)—and then keep building specifics into the character. These are the details that move a character away from generalization and into specificity.

DISCUSSION

For both stories, have students think about the specific qualities each of these characters exhibit. Have them underline places in the text where the students feel the author reveals something about the character.

Writing Exercise

Have your students design a character through a list of specific attributes. Give the character a name, an age, interests (dance, nature, yoga, cars, etc.), "quirks" (maybe they only eat the red Skittles®), and any dominant emotional qualities (maybe they are rigid, or generous, or petty, etc.).

Writing Practice

Using the list from the writing exercise, have students think about something their character wants and something that might be in this character's way of getting it (obstacles can be emotional or external). Next, have them write a 100-word story, titled with their character's name, in which they show this character through specific, unique details.

TIE-IN TO CLASSROOM READING

For whatever current classroom reading your students are doing, have them choose one character and make a list of the specific qualities that make them unique. This exercise encourages them to notice the specific language an author is using to amplify a character and make them more three-dimensional.

3

SETTING

Featured Authors: Haley Johnston, age 16, and Jeff Zentner

REVIEW TERM: character

A story must be housed in a specific world. This is sometimes called "building a world" or creating a "sense of place" in a piece of writing. A setting is made richer through specific sensory detail (more in Chapter 9). Most importantly, a setting isn't static. It can determine things for the character, cause or solve problems for them, or act as an agent of change.

In her story "Paris, Texas" Haley uses both the interior world of the room and the exterior world outside the window to show her character wrestling with what is clearly a betrayal. She also uses the specificity of a named city. She is clever using Paris, *Texas,* and not the more famous City of Light—Haley's Paris is a darker one, indeed. At least for this character.

Paris, Texas

She stared out the window with her arms crossed over her chest. She found the brown landscape comforting. The room's bed was making her sick—it was too similar to his, reminding her of how he'd shared it with someone else.

She watched the sun descend beneath the hills of the Texan wilderness. She welcomed the coming darkness, aware that she had already pushed all those nights with him out of her mind. Only this time, the bright colors of the hotel furniture replaced the bright lights of the city.

"Paris," she scoffed. She hated that city. She hated him.

—HALEY JOHNSTON

Jeff Zentner is an award-winning YA author whose books never fail to tug at our hearts. One way he does this is by directly tying place to significant moments for his characters. Pay close attention to how he uses details about this very specific *spot* to provide the emotional weight of his story "The Spot."

The Spot

"Here?" I ask my dad.

He pauses before answering. He kneels and runs his hand over the tops of the grass and weeds. "Here," he murmurs.

We stand and listen to the buzzing of insects in the close June heat. There's no other sound. This road is sparsely traveled.

I don't want to ask but I do. "Did she suffer?"

"No. Happened too fast."

I sit on the spot. "I wish I knew her."

"Me too."

"Thank you for bringing me here."

He nods and starts to speak but tears fill his eyes and he's silent. He sits beside me.

–JEFF ZENTNER

DISCUSSION

When choosing a setting for a story, an author must consider certain questions. How can the setting best serve the story and what the author wants to write?

1. What are some specifics both authors use to give us a sense of place in these stories?

2. What is significant about each setting for these two stories?

Writing Exercise

1. Have students choose a setting that is meaningful to them (like a baseball park, a beach, a friend's living room, a vacation spot) and write a short description of this place, zeroing in on all five senses: smells, tastes, textures, sounds, visuals. Ask them to be specific!

2. Give students five minutes to create a list of other possible settings. Have them consider interior and exterior settings, including both public and private spaces. Have them try to come up with at least fifteen settings.

3. Next, ask them to place a character in the middle of one of the settings. Encourage students to give this character some action (something to do there) and to write a few lines using the descriptions created in the

first part of this exercise to enhance the activity for this character.

4. Next, ask students to create a scene between two characters and use one of the private spaces on their list (a living room, a car parked on an empty street).

5. Finally, they'll take those two characters and the same conflict/discussion and set this same scene in one of the public spaces on their list (a crowded restaurant, a baseball game). How does this change the interaction between these two characters? How does it stay the same?

Writing Practice

Choosing either the private or public space from the above exercise, have students grow this scenario into a 100-word story where they focus on using the setting to amplify the character's arc.

TIE-IN TO CLASSROOM READING

Have students reflect on other stories they have studied in class so far (novels, short stories, etc.). Using one of these, have them choose a setting they believe amplified a story for a specific character.

4

THE RELATIONSHIP BETWEEN POV, CHARACTER, AND SETTING

Featured Authors: Emma Brink, age 17, and Tara Campbell

REVIEW TERMS: setting, POV, character

As we move through this book, I hope it will become obvious that, while there is value in separating the parts (I'm writing an entire book where I do this!), all these parts work together to build a story. Thus, it's important to study them in relation to each other.

One of my favorite integrated studies is the relationship between POV, character, and setting. A character lives in a body and this body lives in a place. As characters move through places and notice things with specific points of view, we, as readers, begin to know them better.

Here's a story from teen author Emma Brink.

We Regret to Inform You

I stood in front of a Chevron® staring at the greasy door, letter damp in my fist.

"Hey, kid," said a voice behind me, rough like chalk dragged over asphalt. "*Move.*"

I turned, feeling cold seep through my muddied threadbare bunny slippers. His posture was the freshly sharpened edge of a blade. He looked my age, maybe younger. He didn't smile, neither did I.

He noticed the letter, more perceptive than his attitude suggested, sneered, and said: "Screw college. Want a Coke®?"

Accepting drinks from strangers was the kind of thing I'd never do. I nodded and followed him inside.

—EMMA BRINK

That first line! Emma immediately draws us into a place, a character who is wrestling with something, and a specific POV in this single line. We know this character is standing outside of a Chevron (a gas station, with a greasy door, no less) and we know the letter in this character's hand must be important in some way.

DISCUSSION

1. What do we know about these two characters? Underline the details in the story that show us something about each of them.

2. Draw a circle around important setting details that provide a strong sense of place (like that "greasy door").

3. What is the POV? How does this amplify the story?

Before you move into another writing exercise, have students first study this incredible story by award-winning flash fiction author Tara Campbell.

The Greatest Show

We climbed down from our platforms and out of the ring, inhaling deeply of sawdust and popcorn, sweat and dung. We turned out the lights and broke down the tents, ropes biting into our palms. We watered the elephants and fed the lions; we waved at stragglers and kissed our new lovers goodbye. One last campfire, one last harmonica bray, one last cloud of dust kicked up by our dancing feet. One last paycheck pressed into our hands. No train tomorrow. No makeup, no spangled costumes. We'll tip our heads back, way back, and spread our arms for the net.

–TARA CAMPBELL

DISCUSSION

1. Encourage students to notice that cool POV choice in "The Greatest Show" (the collective "we" as the narrator). How does this choice amplify the story in relation to character? Who is this story about?

2. Study the setting. Have students circle the details that show this place.

3. Discuss how these three things—POV, character, place—all work together in service to that final, glorious line. What might she mean by "We'll tip our heads back, way back, and spread our arms for the net"? Where does this leave you as a reader? How does it make you *feel*?

Writing Exercise

I love lists. Anyone who has read my fourth YA novel *The Possibility of Now* knows I built this love of lists into my main character, Mara. She makes lists for everything. Lists are helpful when writing stories too. They can help us come up with original ideas and organize our specific literary elements before writing. This is especially effective for foundational elements like Character and Setting.

"I have nothing to write about . . ."

We've all heard it. That kid wedged into the corner who doesn't much like to make eye contact. The one who turns in a few sentences when you ask for a half page or one sentence when you ask for a paragraph. I like to think of these students as my less-is-more kiddos, my natural haiku writers.

Usually, they need some prompting.

Lists are especially helpful when dealing with the "I don't have anything to write about" brand of young writer in your classroom. When they argue they have "nothing to write about," I give them some list options (see Figure 4.1, also OR5):

> ### List of Lists!
>
> - List everything on your coffee table at home
> - List everything you love about winter (or summer, spring, fall)
> - List some favorite flavors
> - List words you find interesting
> - List characters you like in books and movies
> - List every tree and flower you can think of
> - List different kinds of birds
> - List the smells you like the most
> - List the things that make someone a good friend
> - List the most annoying sounds
> - List the textures you like most
> - List what you might find under the seat of a car
> - List all the things that might make a dog bark
> - List places you would teleport to if you could
> - List your favorite foods and snacks

Figure 4.1

The goal here, of course, is once again specificity. Specific detail shapes fiction. It centers a reader in a specific world with clear features. Lists are also not as daunting as sentences—no tricky subject-verb combos to stress out young writers who aren't quite sure of the shape they want to make out of their sentences yet.

Another fun exercise to do as a whole class is to create "class lists" that you keep on the wall. Lists of specifics—smells, tastes, textures, sounds, sights. This can give our more reluctant writers a place for their eyes to stray when they need inspiration. It can help those students who are already writing long passages to fine-tune their sentences, to use specificity to amplify the worlds they are already building. For example, instead of saying, "Eric had a snack," a writer can remember their list of snacks and write, "Eric ate a bowl of buttered popcorn with sugar sprinkled on it."

Specifics!

Writing Practice

Have your students create a list of ten possible characters and ten possible settings. Give students the challenge of choosing one from each list and attempting a 100-word story in which they use a specific POV to amplify their characters and settings.

5

CONFLICT AND TENSION

Featured Authors: Shayden Eagleheart, age 17, and Julie Valin

REVIEW TERMS: character, tone

Raymond Chandler often gets quoted as saying, "When in doubt, have a man come through a door with a gun in his hand" (1950, 13). While I'm not one to condone violence, his point is well taken. Stories need conflict and tension to create a vibrant plot. To paraphrase the author Sands Hall: ease makes for a nice dinner party, but terrible fiction (2008). Characters need something to push against; thus, there must be something causing obstacles for what the character wants or needs. The most obvious way to create these elements is through external conflict (Chandler's man with the gun), but there are also internal conflicts at play in stories.

Teen author Shayden gives an example of this sort of internal conflict in her story "Even When."

Even When

Even if you are fifteen and on vacation, visiting your dad. Even if your siblings are only three and five, even if your dad said he would "meet you there," even if you go searching and can't find him, even if you are in a foreign country. Even if you are alone at a public pool, even if your siblings can't swim, even if someone gets hurt. Even if, six hours later, your dad arrives and says, "Welcome to parenthood." Even if he tells you to be grateful to be there.

Even then, you want to scream, "I am fifteen."

—SHAYDEN EAGLEHEART

Sometimes, the conflict might only be hinted at in 100-word stories, but the emotional choices of the character give us enough tension to pull us through. In Julie Valin's story, we don't know who this character is talking to, but we know a decision gets made about what this character is willing to tolerate—or not.

Leaving It

"Take it back!" she yelled into her phone in the Save Mart® parking lot. "Take it back—I'm nothing like HER! . . . Take it *back*!" She paced outside her white Mustang®.

The mom nearby hurriedly plunked her toddler in his car seat, tossing her sack of groceries inside, an orange Cheetos® bag peeking over the top so all that showed was *Cheet.* . . .

"Then I'll leave!" she threatened, eyes widened. She stood there looking into her phone like it was a face taking its last breath. Then she jumped in the car—gunned it, and peeled away, making good on her promise.

—JULIE VALIN

DISCUSSION

1. For both stories, have students underline the key places that show conflict for the characters—what creates the central conflict in each piece?

2. For Shayden's story, have students pay special attention to the last line, the one the author places on its own. Shayden uses the crucial word *want*—this character *wants* to scream but the line implies that she doesn't, that she keeps the scream inside—why does this fact create tension, especially at the end of the story?

3. What about the last line of Julie's story? How does that create a landing for the conflict and tension in the story?

Writing Exercise

Imagine *three* different conflicts for Julie's story, using the following questions as inspiration:

Who might HER be?

Why doesn't this character want to be compared to HER?

Who is she talking to?

Writing Practice

Take one of your imagined conflicts from the above exercise and write a new 100-word story that reveals what happens next for this character. The goal is to have the students give her a name and a specific place the character drove to once she left the Save Mart lot. What happened once she got there? Encourage them to explore how they can build on the tension, how they can amplify the conflict through their own imaginations as they further this narrative that Julie started.

TIE-IN TO CLASSROOM READING

What stories are your students reading in class right now? Have them choose a story that has a clear central tension/conflict. Have them free-write about how the author creates this tension in the story and then discuss this as a class.

6

VOICE AND TONE

Featured Authors: Aubrey Cline, age 16, and Tabitha Lawrence

REVIEW TERMS: character, setting

Voice is a tricky concept in writing, and one of the more difficult devices to isolate and pin down. With my own work, the focus on voice most often begins with my characters, with how they see the world, how they notice things, how they interact with their environments and other people. A writer's goal is to show how characters live in their specific bodies, exploring what they want/love/fear. These elements work themselves into the anatomy of the sentences so that, in a way that is tough to pin down and feels a bit like magic, a specific voice emerges. *My* voice, *through* them. It's complex. But I know that the source of this is *me*.

When I work with my students, we spend a great deal of time exploring how we specifically see the world because it helps build our own sense of personal voice. We do this while reading other writers and considering the people who populate the world of a specific story—their motivations, desires, obstacles, etc. in relationship to their immediate and larger worlds. Doing these two things in tandem helps our students develop their own characters in their fiction writing as well as develop their own unique, foundational voices for different types of writing.

Let's look at this example from 16-year-old Aubrey Cline.

Influenced

I shut off my phone, awaiting the Instagram® notification flood. *Faith's Finds Online Thrift* has earned more in four months than my parents ever dreamed of having. And I'm only eighteen.

Vacations never happened for us. We didn't ever venture out of Nevada. Sometimes, Reno was the hotspot.

They don't know I'm leaving.

I will have to escape by myself.

I gather the last of my things. My bag is worth more than three month's rent in this stepping-stone apartment. My silver Mercedes-Benz® smiles back at me from the lot. Whoever said money couldn't buy happiness was a filthy liar.

—AUBREY CLINE

That last line really brings the voice home in this story. There is a tone in it that suggests so much struggle and hard work—so many attempts to change her own circumstances.

Speaking of tone: for me, writers establish a tone in their work through the way they use specific sentence work to reveal a unique voice. Tone comes to the surface when a voice is lyrical, humorous, witty, wry, somber, joyful, mysterious, etc. Of course, it can also be a mix of different tones to create an overall textured feeling for the reader. Tone, at its simplest, is the attitude of the piece.

Writing Exercise

Have students generate a short piece of writing (three to five sentences) using this sentence as the first line:

She hadn't seen him in so long.

Next, have them rewrite what they wrote to create a sad tone, focusing on specific language and sentence structure to enhance this sad tone. Then, when they are done, have them rewrite the passage, changing the tone to one of enthusiasm and excitement. Encourage them to use specific words that amplify this new tone.

Have the class read Tabitha Lawrence's story "Desert, Spring," encouraging students to pay close attention to who the narrator might be talking to and how this works with the sentence choices to create voice and tone in the story.

Desert, Spring

When your mind starts to unfurl itself from the tight fist of grief, the everything of it all threatens to overwhelm you. Suddenly, the world reeks of flowers. The hummingbird-sized moths pollinating them almost make you weep. All that was here before. It was you that was elsewhere, and your sudden sloppy jettison back into the world feels psychedelic.

You begin noticing things again. You remember him calling you a "sparkling iridescent loofa of a soul." You gather epiphanies to tell him, one day. Moments. Small luxuries. Miracles, all of it.

My friend. This side of town has grass. *Grass.*

—TABITHA LAWRENCE

DISCUSSION

Who is the narrator in "Desert, Spring" talking to? How do we know this?

Addressing oneself in the second person can be an interesting way to create a voice that feels distanced, even desperate. This is someone experiencing grief, who might even be coming up to the surface to notice they are experiencing this. Zero in on the line: "You remember him calling you a 'sparkling iridescent loofa of a soul.'" Tabitha does so much work in this line—in the way it amplifies not only the voice of this narrator, but also the specific voice of this remembered friend.

What other lines stand out? Why?

Writing Exercise

Have your students use this exercise to delve into their own specific "you-ness." This exercise is built to encourage them to explore each of their unique writing **voices**. Have them respond to the prompts in Figure 6.1 (also OR8) with whatever creative responses (literal or figurative) come to mind. Encourage them to trust their instincts and be as specific and descriptive as possible.

Exploring Voice

I am the sound of:

My personality is the color of:

My personal theme song would be:

I'm a _____ cookie kind of person.

Never put _____ on my pizza.

My perfect day looks like:

If you open my junk drawer, the first thing you'll see is:

I love the smell of:

I get annoyed or frustrated when:

I want to wrap myself in:

The name of the cartoon character based on me is:

My optimum mood lighting is:

Figure 6.1

Writing Practice

Have students choose a specific tone (playful, humorous, somber, frustrated). See if they can take one of their earlier 100-word stories (or write a new one!) and bring this tone to the surface. I like to tell my students that voice is something we cultivate as writers over time—it doesn't happen right away and isn't always easily identifiable. But it's important for them to look at their own work and ask, "How does this sentence, this paragraph, this story showcase my voice as a writer? What are the specific choices I'm making that feel most like my own?"

7

"THE STAKES"

Featured Authors: Max Tel, age 17, and Stacey Lee

REVIEW TERMS: character and conflict

W hen a story feels flat, it can often be because the stakes aren't high or meaningful enough. Simply put: in a piece of fiction, creating something the character *wants*, and then giving them something *at stake* (what might they lose or gain?) around this want, allows for conflict in a narrative because it invests the character (and hopefully the reader) in the outcome of the story.

Sometimes the stakes are external (three people are trapped in a locked room and are trying to escape), but they can also often be internal, something the character is wrestling with emotionally. Or it can, of course, be a combination of both. Like in the following story by Max Tel. Young adults often wonder about the future; it can be both a source of excitement and worry. In "Teenage Playroom," the main character is struggling not only with this emotional concept, but also with her exterior environment.

Teenage Playroom

She glances at the clock on the wall. Only seven minutes have passed. Why is she desperate to leave? She had belonged here. Around her, her friends are laughing and playing. Again and again, she tries to step into their world, but she can't. No, she won't. Theirs is a child's world, full of jokes and judgments. These games aren't fun anymore, and she wonders how they ever were. Her gaze returns to the clock, and she gets to her feet. It is time. Stepping over the remnants of her past, she frees herself. The door closes softly behind her.

—MAX TEL

Stacey Lee is a bestselling YA author whose book *The Downstairs Girl* (2021) was a Reese's Book Club® selection. She always creates meaningful stakes for her characters in her historical fiction and in "Daddy's Flask."

Daddy's Flask

The huckster shuffled his cards. "Pretty girl like you don't belong in a saloon."

"I'll guess your top card for that flask." Daddy had always kept that flask polished to a high gleam. He'd fallen on hard times after Ma died, but now that I was older, I'd take back what was ours. "You win, I'll give you five dollars."

He cut the deck, then lifted the flask to his fishbone smile. "You're on."

As soon as he picked up the card, I knew. The silver had tarnished, but still told me what I needed to know. "Eight of spades."

—STACEY LEE

DISCUSSION

Have students underline places in the stories that show the reader who the characters are and circle places that show what the characters want. Then discuss:

1. What is the central conflict in both stories? What is causing a problem for the characters?
2. What might these characters lose if they get what they want?
3. What might they gain?
4. In Stacey's story, how do the historical details help amplify the situation?

Writing Exercise

Have the students create a character who wants something but feels stuck or has a specific obstacle in the way. Then, have them write a short description of this character detailing what might be at stake, given these circumstances.

Writing Practice

Have students write a 100-word story that shows a moment of change for the character they created in the previous exercise. Have them start by choosing a specific moment when the character makes a decision that will impact their future.

8

THEME

Featured Authors: Maya Pedersen, age 15, and Pearl Fisher, age 11

REVIEW TERMS: tension, character, POV

I had a college professor who once went on, in his words, "a wee rant about theme." Theme, he argued (over the lip of the water bottle he always seemed to have in hand), was not a judgment or a lesson or a moral or a criticism. It was a single entity—war, love, friendship, betrayal—that acted as a driving force in the novel or story. For some reason, this "wee rant" stuck with me, and any time I'd come across a textbook or essay that listed a theme as "war never solves anything" or "love always wins," I would remember my hydrated professor and his "wee rant." Mostly because of that rant, I have always taught my students the same concept: theme is a driving force in the story, often summed up in one or two words. So, when a student says, "my seventh-grade teacher said theme is the central lesson," I often nod along and say, "That makes sense; in here, we're going to operate around this particular definition of theme. It's not necessarily the right one or the only one, it's just the one we're going to use in this classroom."

Some people might scream, *consistency*! I argue that variation is a meaningful force in an ELA classroom. For me, teaching is an art. We are living things impacted by our own experiences, teaching within a gray-area discipline. The study of writing, of literature, of *story* allows for a certain amount of wiggle room. That's one of the things I love most about it (and what many of my students often find most frustrating). "Wait"—that same former student had frowned—"but I learned it this other way."

I tell my students that flexible thinking is part of learning how to be a critical thinker. I believe teaching students how to synthesize various definitions, how to sift through them to find meaning, how to hold two different ideas in tandem, is part of the point. It certainly is for my teaching. To use a famous "general observation" from F. Scott Fitzgerald: "The test of a first-rate intelligence is the ability to hold two opposed ideas in the mind at the same time, and still retain the ability to function" (1936, 41). In an ELA classroom, I think it's key we also hold similar (but slightly changed) definitions next to each other as a way of thinking about story.

In this book, I might give something a different definition from the one you've taught in your classroom. I think that's fine. It's *good*, actually. Let's keep asking our students to evolve their own thinking too.

What might be the themes in "And I Love Her" by Maya Pedersen, and "Sea Witch" by Pearl Fisher?

And I Love Her

I used to drape myself over your bed, mesmerized by your lips moving over glinting silver braces.

I remember splashing cold water on my face after tracing constellations through the freckles on your cheeks.

We'd borrow your dad's record player and listen to David Bowie® on the good days and The Beatles® on the bad ones.

Flipping through magazines with dog-eared pages, we talked for hours. Mostly about how we were going to escape this town, or travel to tropical tourist destinations. Only one of us ever did.

I wish I'd told you I loved you before you were gone.

—MAYA PEDERSEN

Sea Witch

Every morning at dawn, she walked the shore. Her silk dress was the color of the sea. She had no name, but the people in our neighborhood called her the Sea Witch. She wore no shoes, and her long hair was always undone. Every day, I watched her being pulled deeper into the water, gradually, as if she might not even have known, until one day a look of fear crossed her normally peaceful face. Her silk dress had become waves. I leaned forward, watching, then an expression of pure courage took over. The water surged around her. She dived.

—PEARL FISHER

DISCUSSION

1. What seem to be the central themes in these stories? What clues show you these themes?

2. Who is the narrator in each story? How does the point of view inform the theme?

3. What specific words, phrases, or imagery do Maya and Pearl use to create tension in their stories?

Writing Exercise

1. Have your students create a list of ten themes they care about: friendship, betrayal, love, etc.

2. When they are done brainstorming, have each student add a theme that isn't already there to a large sheet of paper (if you want to keep it to display) or on the board.

Writing Practice

Have each student choose a theme from the classroom list and use it as the **title** of a 100-word story in which they develop a character (with a specific POV), setting, conflict, etc. Encourage them to create a story that *shows* this theme in a specific, detailed way.

TIE-IN TO CLASSROOM READING

Have students discuss themes they are seeing in any other reading done so far in class. Do your students see any themes that keep emerging in all stories? Why might this be?

noticing." We are noticing the specific se... noticing the way people interact with each other, th... noticing all the small, bright specific things that mak... breaking. This noticing (and the specific choices we... brant worlds in small spaces, and these worlds begin... have your students practice noticing their worlds... my students. I share it with them as an online docum... it from the online resources. Over the years, man... much of writing is about "seeing"—about noticin... smell, taste, touch, sound. For this assignm... approximately thirty minutes noticing e... about what you see, smell, taste, touch... vignette; they can be just words... you discover in that place, but al... reason I refer to these 100-w... rm is its attention to detail thr... the introduction to this... tell a story through a... gaps of text rather... rticular way beca... hat in all writin... noticing the s... teract with... ht specific... (and the... all spa... its p... vit!

logic of the form is its... As Grant Faulkner wrote... a story, not its sprawl. I had... instead of the layers of a backsto... way because each one must do so much... ents that in all writing (not just with... noticing." We are noticing the specific... are noticing the way people interact with ea... (or don't); we are noticing all the small, bright... utiful and interesting and heartbreaking. This n... because of it) allows us to create unique, vibrant... 's begin at the sentence level. Before starting th... as an online document. You could do the s... m as an online document. You could do the s... sources. Over the years, many of my writ... ting is about "seeing"—about noticing t... r, smell, taste, touch, sound. For t... and spend approximately thirty... here, jot down notes about t... o be complete sentences 0... to try to record the uniq... ime just noticing—look... rd stories as "small... to detail, the prec... uction to t... tell a b...

each one must do... a writer is always "noticin... n each other, the way they spea... eresting and heartbreaking. This n... aces, and these worlds begin at the se... ework assignment I give my students... urces. o...

PART TWO

ELEMENTS OF LANGUAGE

Writing Is Noticing

Part of the reason I refer to these 100-word stories as "small, bright things" is that much of the magic of the form is its attention to detail, the precision that is required of so few words. As Grant Faulkner wrote in the introduction to this book: "I had to find the essence of a story, not its sprawl. I had to learn how to tell a story through a simple detail, a hint, instead of the layers of a backstory. I had to work with the gaps of text rather than stuffing things in to fill the gaps." Authors must choose each word in such a particular way because each one must do so much work to create a full story.

I like to tell my students that in all writing (not just with this form, but with *all* writing), a writer is always "noticing." We are noticing the specific senses that allow us to experience our world; we are noticing the way people interact with each other, the way they speak to each other (or don't); we are noticing all the small, bright *specific* things that make our world beautiful and interesting and heartbreaking. This noticing (and the specific choices we make because of it) allows us to create unique, vibrant worlds in small spaces, and these worlds begin at the sentence level.

Before starting this section, have your students practice noticing their worlds. Below, see the homework assignment I give my students. I share it with them as an online document. You could do the same, or you could download it from the online resources (OR11).

The Art of Noticing

Over the years, many of my writing teachers have talked about how much of writing is about "seeing"—about noticing the sensory details in the world: the way things appear, smell, taste, touch, sound.

For this assignment, I want you to find three different locations and spend approximately thirty minutes noticing each one for its specific details. While there, jot down notes about what you see, smell, taste, touch, hear. These notes don't have to be complete sentences or a full vignette; they can be just words and phrases. The goal is to try to record the unique sensory details you discover in that place, but also to spend time just noticing—looking around, soaking it in.

Location #1:

Location #2:

Location #3:

9

SENSORY LANGUAGE/ SPECIFIC DETAIL

Featured Authors: Alex Belles, age 15, and Darien Hsu Gee

REVIEW TERMS: character, setting

Specific, sensory detail is at the heart of rich writing. It's what moves a story from telling to showing. If you haven't yet had your students complete the Art of Noticing assignment mentioned in the introduction of this section (see page 42 or OR11), you can have them do a truncated version of it in your classroom. Or (if you have an understanding admin who doesn't mind you wandering around school) you can take their writing on the road and walk with them around campus to do this exercise.

As students notice their world, they can write their observations as sentences or as a list. You might ask:

* What are you smelling, tasting, touching, seeing, hearing?

* What are some specific words you can use to describe this world?

These small, sensory specifics are what build a vivid sense of place, a rich character, a clear POV, and a *showing* kind of story. Through their specificity, they amplify each of the foundational pieces we studied in Part One.

Once your students have done this pre-work, have them read the following two stories, "Victory" by teen author Alex Belles, and "Sous" by award-winning author Darien Hsu Gee, paying close attention to the way both authors use specific sensory detail.

Victory

A silver sky poured rain on the rooster's head. From the darkness, burning eyes challenged him. He wailed into the thundering night.

The fox met eyes with the brave old bird. One of us dies tonight. Skin barely stretched over her bones and her squealing pup's cries echoing internally, she ran. One lone hen snagged on the fence. The fiery canine raced the rooster to the weak bird. The rooster kicked the fence, freeing his beloved.

Scars were slashed in the fox's face, the rooster's belly was gashed. That bloody night, the pups ate and the hens slept safe.

Victory.

—ALEX BELLES

Sous

During the pandemic, I am anxious about my kids. One night I make a salsa to accompany the chicken tamales steaming in the rice cooker. I find bulbs of shallots forgotten in the back of the fridge, tender beneath their papery skin. A jar of pickled jalapeños. Cherry tomatoes the size of ping pong balls, still on the vine. Fresh cilantro from the garden, even though the plant has bolted. A grind of sea salt.

My 14-year-old son takes a spoonful. "Wow," he says. "It's good, mom."

I was holding my breath. I was worried it might not be enough.

—DARIEN HSU GEE

DISCUSSION

1. For both stories, have students underline places that feel the most specific in sensory detail.

2. Ask them why they chose these places in the story.

3. Ask them what they notice about how the specifics make the story stronger.

4. Point out to the students that titles can also make a story more specific. "Sous" can mean *underneath*. How does this title amplify the story?

Writing Exercise

1. Have students revisit the places they noticed from their earlier assignment, whether that was the Art of Noticing three places assignment or the classroom/campus observation.

2. Ask them to choose one of these places.

3. Now, ask them to create a character living in that setting who has a problem or is experiencing a moment of change.

Writing Practice

1. Have students write a 100-word story about the character from their writing exercise.

2. When they finish a working draft, have them underline the places where they have been most specific in terms of their five senses. Ask them: Are there places that could be improved by including more specific sensory images? Have them look for places where they might have used a general word like "tree," and can make it more specific by naming it "a maple tree."

10

IMAGERY

Featured Authors: Julia Allgeyer, age 14, and Kirsten Casey

REVIEW TERM: setting

I don't know about you, but I have certain lessons I turn to year after year that just continue to show up for me as an ELA teacher. One of the lessons I've been using since I started teaching in 1997 is a lesson on the difference between figurative and literal imagery in poetry and other types of descriptive writing.

I give the students the following two definitions:

> ***Literal Image:*** *an image that aims to replicate in words the object or experience; the subject is recreated realistically; and*

> ***Figurative Image:*** *an image that likens an object or experience to something else, sometimes surprising or different.*

To prepare for the lesson, I have them fold a piece of white drawing paper in half. I make sure they have colorful pens, crayons, or pencils close at hand.

In the past, I've had them read two poems: "Nantucket" by William Carlos Williams and "Metaphors" by Sylvia Plath. For this book,

Nevada County Poet Laureate Kirsten Casey (who is also one of our story editors) wrote two poems for you to use in your classroom (but you can also Google™ those other two if you'd like).

Kirsten wrote "Power Outage" as a poem rooted in literal imagery (of course, because she's Kirsten she couldn't help but add that one figurative line in the landing). As your students read, have them underline literal images:

Power Outage

The trees crisscross with the live wires,
their X's leaving us without lights, without heat,
without phones. The tracks
in the deep snow vary in size: workboots,
doe hooves, the trail of a pulled sled.
We shake heavy branches, shovel paths, hope
for news of restored power, clear roads.
My cold morning breath no different than
the breath of the crow in its nest.
But the crow is already collecting glossy treasures
the plow overturned: a strand of silver
tinsel from a bag of New Year's trash, a torn
envelope lined in gold foil, and
a broken pomegranate, its scattered
arils like drops of blood across the snow.

—KIRSTEN CASEY

For Kirsten's figurative example, she wrote "Tonight" as a poem rooted almost exclusively in figurative imagery. As your students read, have them underline places where she uses figurative imagery—where images represent not only their actual meaning, but also are likened to something else.

Tonight

the sky is like an empty mouth filling

with cold water, like a painting

of a black mirror covered

in attic dust. The stars are as absent

as tombs that flood, where the dead

float away in cloudy water, only

to freeze and thaw miles

downstream. I smell the dirty

ice, the factory exhaust, the wood burning

fire smoke, wide plumes like black ribbons

in the air, unwinding through the white, writing

on it like paper. Creating

and dissolving, creating

and dissolving. The clouds taste

chalky and useless, like sampling

what is erased, the pale powder

in the tin tray of an empty schoolhouse.

The wind is not the wind

without the tree branches, without

the objects it pushes against. The wind

is an invisible bully on a playground.

The wind pokes holes in the clouds, rearranges

the lowest stars, finds itself trapped

in old shutter hinges, loose chimney bricks,

that crack in the basement window. The land

below me spreads out like last

thoughts, an immeasurable vista, stretching wide

with expectation, and then later,

inevitably, ending in regret.

—**KIRSTEN CASEY**

Once students have read the poems, I have them label one side of their paper with "Nantucket"/"Power Outage" and one side of their paper with "Metaphors"/"Tonight" and ask them, to the best of their abilities (no pressure, they've seen *my* artwork!), to draw each poem as if someone has taken a photograph of it (they can use their underlines for guidance). I allow a significant amount of time for this, sometimes as much as twenty minutes, depending on how engaged they are with the task of drawing.

After they are done with their pictures, I have them hold up only the side of their picture for "Nantucket"/"Power Outage" as a group and we make observations as a class.

1. What images did we all use?

2. What colors are present in all our pictures?

3. What is the setting?

4. What does this tell us about this poem in relation to imagery?

Next, I have students hold up the other side, the picture for "Metaphors"/"Tonight" and we make more observations as a class:

1. What images did we all use? Did we all draw these in the same way?

2. What are the similarities about our pictures?

3. What are the differences?

4. What does this tell us about this poem in relation to imagery?

Over my two decades using this lesson, students have for the most part discovered the same thing: all the literal drawings appear pretty much the same while the figurative poem is full of distinction and interpretation.

It's a quick visual explanation of the difference between literal and figurative imagery.

Imagistic writing allows us as readers to "see" a piece of writing; it helps build specific details and sensory language so that we can live in the world of the story or poem.

Teen author Julia Allgeyer wrote the following 100-word story to capture a moment during the pandemic. As your students read it, have them use two different-colored pencils to underline images that feel literal and images that feel figurative.

Sunrises

The sun dips below the horizon on this dreary night. The moon, weary from her endless chase, rests in a nest of stars, out of sight. The night sky blankets sleepy towns like thick, wet snow; it suffocates everything beneath it. The people, small tendrils of fear, are afraid to step outside. There is no telling who is sick. It could be anyone, anywhere. Locked in their own homes, the people sit.

Alone.

The dark provides no solace from despair. But just when the night becomes too heavy to bear, sunrays pierce the shadows surrounding lonely hearts.

Hope seeps in.

—JULIA ALLGEYER

DISCUSSION

Did everyone mark the same things? Why or why not?

Writing Exercise

1. Have students think about some of their favorite places and the images associated with those places.

2. Have them choose one place and create a list of images they associate with that place. Remind them that images are sensory, and to make sure they are employing all five senses.

Writing Practice

Have the students write an imagistic 100-word story in which they focus on employing both literal and figurative images, with an emphasis on the setting.

Depending on how much time you want to devote to this lesson, two follow-up/add-on lessons could include:

1. Having a partner "draw" the author's story

2. Having the author create a collage that represents their story and placing the story in the center of the collage (these look really pretty on the walls of your classroom—great assignment for back-to-school-night displays).

11

SYMBOLISM

Featured Authors: Isabel Yang, age 13, and Kasie West

REVIEW TERMS: sensory language, imagery

Symbolism is when something in the text—an object, a color, weather, etc.—stands for more than just its literal meaning, amplifying the story and giving it deeper meaning for the reader. I want to stress this last part: *for the reader.* I've always felt, as an author, that once my story is out in the world it starts belonging to its readers.

Besides, sometimes readers see things I didn't know I was doing, at least not intentionally. A student once asked me, "But did the author really *mean* it like that, or are you just being a *total English teacher* about it?" Which made me laugh. I told her, "Maybe both?" But she's not wrong: I was being a total English teacher about it.

And, yes, sometimes it's both. The author did mean it that way. *And* the reader read it that way. But sometimes it's something only the reader saw clearly. Sometimes, the author might not have sat there and thought, "I am writing this tree to symbolize growth," but it doesn't mean we can't *see* it that way as readers. I recall sitting in a college class many years ago and listening to my professor wax poetic about the symbolism of the final image of a window and moon in a story I'd written. "Kim uses this window as a symbol of hope," he told our class. "She *ends* the story with this character looking toward this window, to that sliver of moon outside. Things were *dire* for this character," he elaborated, "but there is *HOPE*. That window, and the slice of moon through it." As I listened to him, I remember thinking: *Did I do that? Was that what I meant?* Turns out, it actually was what I meant; I just hadn't totally realized it when I was writing. So even if I didn't think about my symbolism as I was crafting that final image, it was what I was trying to convey with the story's ending. I wanted it to land with a feeling of hope. These days, I think I'm more aware of what I'm doing in my writing, but at the time it was just lovely to see the class explore possibilities in my work, for me to see that my choices mattered.

Let's look at how seventh grader Isabel Yang uses a meaningful object to create emotional symbolism in her story "The Firefly Jar."

The Firefly Jar

We sat beneath the stars every night. Glass jars in hand, together we caught fireflies, luminous specks against the dark blanket of evening. Our laughter filled the field time and again.

Until one night, it didn't.

I came alone. Sorrow, a suffocating cloak, hung over the silence. Before sealing the last cardboard box, she'd slipped me her firefly jar. It seemed to glow with memories. I'd clutched it tightly long after her car disappeared.

Now, tears trickled down my face. Fireflies only live one day in a jar. In the meadow grass, I gently opened it and let them go.

—**ISABEL YANG**

DISCUSSION

1. What does the firefly jar symbolize for this character?

2. What specific images does Isabel use to amplify the meaning of the jar?

Now examine how big-hearted YA author Kasie West evolves the symbol of the neighborhood fence separating these two characters in her 100-word story "Fences."

Fences

"What?" she whispered in the space between the two planks of wood, sure she'd heard him wrong.

The fence between their yards had felt like a barrier most of her life. The nuisance that stood in the way of kickball and hide 'n seek, after-school swims and late-night lightning bug searches. Fences make good neighbors, people say. But not when her neighbor was her best friend.

Now, the fence stood between them tall and strong like protection. It smelled like cedar and hope . . . or fear. His breath touched her cheeks. Her heart picked up speed.

"I'm in love with you."

—**KASIE WEST**

DISCUSSION

1. How does the symbolism of Kasie's fence change over the story for these characters?

2. What specific details does Kasie use to do this?

Writing Exercise

Have students make a list of at least ten potential meaningful objects.

Writing Practice

1. Have students choose one of their objects from the exercise above and make it the title of a 100-word story.

2. As they write, encourage them to use sensory language to show how this object is *meaningful* for one to two characters. This vivid imagery can help grow the tension and the stakes for the characters and this object can be a meaningful force for that.

12

ACTIVE LANGUAGE

Featured Authors: Rose, age 17, and Jessica Taylor

REVIEW TERMS: symbolism, voice, specific detail

As writers, our word choices matter. Active language means choosing specific words and syntax to best keep sentences, paragraphs, and, ultimately, whole stories engaging to the reader. It creates that elusive phrase we often hear—"the flow" of a piece. Quick, crisp lines will create a rhythm different from elongated, lyrical sentences, but both can be *active*. I don't have a specific chapter in this book devoted to pacing, but active language is one of the many things that determines the energy and order of a scene. Active language means choosing specific words that create vivid pictures of the world the characters live in.

I like to tell my students that they need to crawl into their stories and walk around in their sentences to pay close attention to the language they are using. This ultimately helps them amplify their own voice work in writing.

Let's walk around in the sentences that 17-year-old Rose chose for her 100-word story.

Dump Jason

You're too good for Jason. Don't get me wrong; he's a great guy. I love that he's friends with Ryan. Great for double dates. And you're both weird; I mean that as a compliment. Seriously, though, Melissa; yesterday he leapt in front of a moving motorcycle!

And he never cleans up after himself. Once, I watched him spit cherry pits onto a cutting board and leave them there. Who does he think cleans that up?

Anyway, I support whatever, but even Ryan said you're too smart for him. And that was before he flung himself in front of that motorcycle.

—ROSE

Now, have your students pay close attention to how award-winning YA author Jessica Taylor uses active language to amplify the voice of her character, especially around the symbol of this specific tree.

Places that Know You

The tree in my yard is a brown husk of summers before. It looks lonely out my window, balded by my dad in an attempt to stop an orange-and-red blanket from choking our lawn. We used to crash through those autumn leaves like they were waves. Those branches still hang halfway over the redwood fence that used to be yours. Last summer, they cracked and whimpered under our weights as we climbed to the tip top. Moving trucks are good at carrying things away—pots, pans, your mom's sewing machine. Not the sound of your feet scrambling up that trunk.

—JESSICA TAYLOR

DISCUSSION

1. Where in each of these stories is the language most active?

2. Have students underline the places where they felt each author was most active in her choices, and share with the group.

3. How do these specific choices magnify the voice of each character?

4. In Jessica's story, what is the symbolism of the tree? How does her specific language create this symbol?

Writing Exercise

Have your students open their portfolios and choose one of the 100-word stories they've written so far to investigate their own active language.

1. Ask them: Where are you most active? Where are the word choices vivid, specific, dynamic?

2. Ask them: where could you choose more active language?

Writing Practice

This is a wonderful opportunity for revision, an essential part of any writing practice. Have your students revise their stories, considering how they can make the language in each sentence more active, more dynamic. Have them walk around in their own sentences.

More on revision later in Part Four of this book!

13

DIALOGUE

Featured Authors: Penelope Johnson, age 17, and Amy Rutten

REVIEW TERMS: symbolism, tension

G ood dialogue can do so much work in a story, especially at the sentence level. It can shape pacing, advance the plot, and drop readers into the specific voice of a certain character outside of the POV. It can provide an immediacy to a certain moment because that specific character speaks those words at a specific time. As readers, when we hear dialogue, we can feel present in the scene with these characters—we are literally eavesdropping on them.

Let's explore the way Penelope uses dialogue to ground the end of her symbolic story.

Grief's Choice

A man slumps on the bench of the Grief City Station, watching the train from Loss screech to a stop. Among its glassy-eyed passengers, one woman stumbles forth, fighting with her stroller and suitcase to find the ticket in her purse. She places the ticket in the stroller. The man follows her gaze to another train, seconds from departure. Abandoning her bags, she rushes the stroller onto it, placing a kiss and tear on the baby's head.

"Where's your baby going?" he asks her.

"Heaven. Where are you going?"

"Death. And you?"

She smiles. "Recovery. Would you come with me?"

—PENELOPE JOHNSON

Sometimes, dialogue is a way to reveal story. In librarian and author Amy Rutten's story, the dialogue shows not only the dynamic, strange world the characters find themselves in, but also a hint at why they might be there in the first place.

Under the Rainbow

"Wait," I said, grabbing Ozmund's arm before he could step off of the spaceship's ramp onto the emerald-green surface of the Goldilocks planet. "Look."

A perfect rainbow, no higher than Ozmund's ankle, shimmered above the miniature forest of microgreens that covered the landscape. I lowered myself to my knees and squinted at a subtle movement beneath the canopy. With a trembling finger, I parted the plants. A group of tiny humanoid creatures huddled beneath, staring at us in fear.

"My God!" I whispered. "We're giants!"

"Then we must learn to tread lightly," Ozmund said, "for this is our last chance."

—AMY RUTTEN

DISCUSSION

1. What is symbolic in both stories?

2. How do the authors use their dialogue to further the tension of the story?

3. What are the strongest lines of dialogue in each story?

Writing Exercise

Dialogue can also add tension in a scene because what a character says and what that character might be thinking could be two different things. When this happens, only the reader sees that tension fully. Have your students do the following exercise, exploring how a character might say one thing, but think something different. (This also creates subtext–more to come in Chapter 16.)

When I was a high school theater teacher, I used to do a game called "Neutral Scenes." I would give my actors some very basic dialogue like the following:

A: Hi

B: Oh, hey.

A: So, how are you?

B: Fine. (pause) You?

A: You know.

B: Of course.

A: Where are you off to?

B: The same old place.

Then, I would give the actors some information (you two used to be friends but you had a fight a few weeks ago and haven't spoken since *or* you two are both interviewing for a promotion at the job where you have both worked for ten years, etc.). The information changes how they say the lines.

We do this as authors too because, depending on the POV, we get to write the interiority of a scene so the reader might know things that one of the characters doesn't know. This can create interesting tension and the dialogue can work overtime.

For this exercise, have your students name A and B in the above scene and then, using the dialogue, write the interior thoughts of one or both of these characters as well as their physical actions during the scene.

Writing Practice

Have your students write a 100-word story made up mostly of dialogue and interior thought, where we see at least one of the characters saying one thing but thinking something else.

14

THE FIRST LINE—THE WINDOW INTO THE WORLD

Featured Author: Rain Skyler, age 17

REVIEW TERMS: active language (specifically through repetition), tone

The first line of a story is the reader's window into the world. It must do a lot of work, and should be meaningful to the overall tone of the story that will follow. Check out Rain's first line in the story "Baby Bat" to see how he pulls the reader into this world.

Baby Bat

In this moment I should feel afraid.

But I don't as I watch the golden rays reach for the tree line. It doesn't burn yet. And I can't make myself feel fear. Because there is the sun, and it's so warm. And it doesn't burn yet.

And all this time they said it was a punishment from the divine. That it would burn just to look at it. But I am seeing this soft glowing light and they're wrong.

It saddens me knowing they'll go the rest of eternity hiding from the sun. . . .

When maybe it doesn't burn at all.

—RAIN SKYLER

DISCUSSION

1. How does the first line of Rain's story set the scene? How does it provide a window to the rest of the story?

2. Have students underline two places in the story that made them wonder something about this character and place. Share the findings with the group.

3. Have students circle two or three specific details in the story that provide clues to the question: What about the setting might cause conflict for this character?

4. What do we know about this character? What are some specific details that show this?

5. Why is "burn" an example of active language? What tone does its repetition create in the story? Have students discuss how Rain builds this tension throughout the story.

Writing Exercise

Have students practice making a list of six to eight compelling first lines. Encourage them to jot down whatever comes to mind, no matter how strange or unexpected it may be (sometimes those strange flashes of inspiration lead to the most interesting stories). They will use these for their writing practice in the next chapter.

TIE-IN TO CLASSROOM READING

For the classroom novel or a book of their choice, have students look closely at the first lines of three to four chapters. Are these good examples of "windows" into the story? How so?

15

"THE LANDING"— THE POWER OF THE LAST LINE

Featured Authors: Ana Sagebiel, age 16, and Ran Walker

REVIEW TERMS: first lines, the stakes, symbolism

A s with the hook of the first line and the window it creates into a story, the power of the last line should provide a satisfying ending, or "landing" of the story. Everything in the story leads up to this moment and it is our job as writers to make it count. Have your students read the story "The Human Algorithm," written by teen author Ana Sagebiel, with particular attention to that last line.

The Human Algorithm

They picked her up in Los Angeles from a failed commercial job, desperate for a role. Her bags were packed for her. There was a car driving by, the exhaust smelling slightly of bubblegum.

Just one more thing they had gotten wrong about Earth.

Her polka dot dress fit just right. The room was clean, maybe too clean. Everything seemed normal. They promised this was the last role she would ever have to play: Caucasian woman, 32, lower-end job. She was there to fill a space. She sighed faintly, smoothing her already ironed dress.

She missed the smell of gas.

—ANA SAGEBIEL

DISCUSSION

1. Have students underline two places in the story that made them wonder something about this character and place. Share the findings with the group.

2. Have students circle two to three specific details in the story that provide clues to the idea that something about this world might be strange.

3. What do we know about the main character? What are some specific details that show this?

4. Who might "they" be? What details from the story support this theory?

5. Have students look closely at that last line. How does it land for them? How does it wrap up the rest of the story to give it a clear beginning, middle, and end (arc)?

6. What might be the significance of the title?

Now let's look at this piece by award-winning author Ran Walker, paying close attention to his first and last lines, which truly bookend his spectacular story "Rainbow."

Rainbow

When Tony promised he'd bring a rainbow to school on Friday, no one believed him—except Alisha, who was known to believe in such things.

When Friday came, nearly everyone in the schoolyard gathered around him during recess, their collective curiosity as thick as a malt milkshake, all of them watching his clasped hands.

"Stand back," Tony said, turning his face away in anticipation.

His hands shot open and seven colors leaped from his palms in an august arch.

The kids, nearly blinded, gasped in astonishment, but only Alisha stood there, smiling, her sunglasses having already been put in place.

—RAN WALKER

DISCUSSION

1. How do Ran's first and last lines play off each other?

2. What is at stake for these characters in this story? How does the landing magnify this?

3. What might the rainbow symbolize?

Writing Practice

Have the students use the list of possible first lines they wrote in their exercise from Chapter 14. Choosing one, have them write an original 100-word story set in an unusual place or centered around an unusual, even magical, idea. Have them focus on creating a last line that reveals something—either about the character, the world itself, or both.

TIE-IN TO CLASSROOM READING

For the classroom novel or a book of their choice, have students look closely at both the first and last lines of three to four chapters. Are these good examples of windows into the story? Are the landings effective for these chapters? Why or why not?

16

BACKSTORY AND SUBTEXT

Featured Authors: Dylan Gibson, age 15, and Darcy Woods

REVIEW TERMS: the stakes, dialogue, POV, conflict

Even if information doesn't eventually come out in the final draft, it helps if an author knows the backstory of a character so they can understand and convey what this character wants in the narrative. As writers, when we know a character's history, inner thoughts, dreams, ideas, etc., it allows us to show some of those elements through the character's behaviors and thoughts. When we know a character's backstory, we may utilize subtext in a scene (the emotions, ideas, wants) beneath a verbalized line. This helps to create conflict and tension; it helps keep the stakes vital.

As readers, we often don't know a character's entire backstory (*especially* in a 100-word story), but it is useful if the writer does. Knowing our characters' backstories indirectly makes the writing richer and more engaging, because anything we write is informed by this knowledge.

Teen author Dylan Gibson peppers her story "Murmurations" with inferences about this character's backstory to create the central conflict.

Murmurations

I saw a crow dive-bomb a murmuration of starlings over the cemetery today. Mom's always said that seeing the flocks prophesied luck, but as I leaned against the chain-link fence on the highway overpass, those little birds of hope scattered. I've never believed in omens. That was Mom's job. And yet, her predictions always came true.

I shivered against the wind, still staring at the birds. I was freezing. God, why did I spend all of my money on a knock-off jacket that didn't keep me warm? I only bought it because I liked the tag: "Soft as mother's hug."

—DYLAN GIBSON

YA author Darcy Woods also explores a mother–daughter relationship of a different sort with a complicated backstory in "More Than a Waitress."

More Than a Waitress

I skipped school. Lied to my parents. Drove 158 miles.

All for this moment.

I'm a hurricane of emotions, waiting for the waitress to notice the matching constellations of copper flecks in our eyes. Our shared dimples. Our—

"Know what you want?" she impatiently repeats.

But . . . she *must* know. Mother's instinct? We were connected once, by a tiny, life-giving cord.

Fantasy collides with the cold reality of her empty stare.

"Nothing," I blurt, like the stranger I am.

What I want can't be found at Last Drop Diner. Maybe it was always in the one place I didn't look.

Home.

—DARCY WOODS

DISCUSSION

1. For both stories, have students underline places where the character infers a backstory.

2. As readers, what are we told outright and what must we infer?

3. How do these inferences help shape the stakes of each story?

4. How do both writers use specific backstory details to create a sense of conflict in their stories?

Writing Exercise

Let's go back to the neutral scene described in Chapter 13 (see page 63):

A: Hi

B: Oh, hey.

A: So, how are you?

B: Fine. (pause) You?

A: You know.

B: Of course.

A: Where are you off to?

B: The same old place.

Depending on the backstory, these lines can mean many different things. Let's consider a possible scenario. Let's assume these two characters were good friends in middle school but have been getting frustrated with each other since they started at a new high school. Character A feels like Character B is always in the drama room. Character B feels like Character A is making new friends in the art program and not including her. Right before this scene, Character A was supposed to meet Character B at the drama room entrance, but she forgot. Actors could show all of this through their performances. As writers, we must show it through interiority (what a character is thinking) and behaviors (what a character is doing).

For this example (Figure 16.1), we are in Character A's POV.

She finds me in the art room, pressing her face to the window.

I wave but go back to working on my drawing. "Hi," I say when she comes into the room.

She raises her eyebrows, her face flushed. "Oh, hey."

I scratch charcoal across the page. "So, how are you?"

She looks like she's about to say something. "Fine." I feel her lean toward me. "You?"

I scratch harder across the paper. "You know."

"Of course." She pushes away from the table, shaking her head.

I can't believe she is leaving. Doesn't she want to stay and talk to me about everything? "Where are you off to?"

She turns, hands on her hips. "The same old place." She pushes back through the door that has barely had time to close and disappears.

Figure 16.1

1. Have your students write this whole scene from the other character's POV.

2. Have your students take the dialogue and create an entirely different backstory for it.

Writing Practice

Have students write a new 100-word story that uses subtext to infer things about the characters' backstory, *or* choose one of the stories from their portfolios and see if they can infuse it with more backstory/subtext.

Creating a Culture of Personal Voice in Readers and Writers: Part One

In 2017, I had the opportunity to speak at a social-emotional learning conference in Honolulu hosted by Marnie Masuda-Cleveland, executive director of the Creative Core. Much of that talk provided the foundation for what I'm going to write about for both parts of this essay, mostly because these issues continue to come up for me as an ELA teacher.

I believe the evolution of personal voice in writing so often blooms alongside the acknowledgment of what we value in our practices as readers and story consumers. Too often, school can become a place where young readers learn to dislike reading, rather than a place where their own connections to the written word grow. Perhaps this happens because of a lack of connection to the authors/stories teachers give their students. Regardless of why it happens, I think we can take steps to avoid that in our classrooms by centering on a respect for the development of personal voice.

Most years, whether I'm teaching English or Creative Writing or both, I begin by having my students create a list. On this list, they write names of books, music, movies, video games, board games, and any other form of media or entertainment or storytelling that has importance for them. I called it the "Stories I Love" list. This introductory exercise allows me some insight into these new teenagers sitting at tables in my room, but it is also a way for me to begin teaching them the power of connecting to voices other than their own. Some years ago, I read a list from a young man who hadn't mentioned a single book. He was clearly passionate about worlds—he listed the Marvel® movies and *Lord of the Rings*® series as movies that spoke to him. But not a single book. After class the next day, I approached him. "So no books on your list?" He looked slightly embarrassed and said, "I'm not a reader." "That's okay," I assured him. "We'll work on that in here." But then something interesting happened. He went on to say, "I mean, I don't read *school* books. I figured you'd want me to list serious books. I read a lot of sci-fi and fantasy." "Like what?" I asked him. He thought about it and listed some series I'd heard of and some I hadn't. "Except," he told me, again apologetically, "now I'm in high school and I don't like any of the school books."

What's interesting to me about this story is not that he didn't feel connected to the books we read in school (this happens all the time, and for the record, I'm a fan of students sometimes reading books they don't want to read). Rather, what struck me was how apologetically this young man insisted he *wasn't* a reader. Somehow, somewhere, he grew to have the impression that there were books you listed to a teacher to show yourself as a reader, and books you kept to yourself that didn't qualify you as one. This suggested that he'd learned somewhere along the way that certain books weren't of value. It got me thinking about the unspoken (or sometimes loud and clear) ways we diminish a person as a reader based on their choices and our own biases. The ways we make them feel like what they're reading doesn't have enough value to be considered "real" reading.

I think this is a shame, and for me it has happened far too often with my students (and, honestly, many of my friends). Much of what I hope as a teacher of both writing and reading is to encourage my students to see the stories they love as connections to outside voices, voices other than their own, that they *value*.

This identification is essential to growing a writing voice.

In 2009, I had the opportunity to sit in conversation with Ethan Canin, a novelist I *adore*, as part of a program called Wordslingers. In his talk with us, he said that when we read, we are reaching our hand out into the universe to shake the hand of another sensibility. Sometimes, we feel nothing in this handshake, sometimes we feel everything connecting, and sometimes it's in between. This connection tells us something. Through it, readers not only start to build their understanding of the larger world and its themes, but also identify their own specific values. My beloved high school English teacher, Mike Cartan, explained it this way: "With every book you read, hold it up to your heart and mind and see what matches" (2007). He and Ethan Canin present similar ideas here.

In May of 2018, novelist Matt Haig blogged for Waterstones® bookstore, writing that stories are essential because "reading is love in action." I love the active quality of this expression. This concept is the driving force behind why books (*all* books) matter. The other term I use a lot (and for the life of me, can't remember where it is from!) is the idea of books as "empathy engines"—of books as made up of moving parts that generate thoughtfulness and insight and empathy. A powerful force indeed.

To grow their own writing voice, students need to connect with written voices they can relate to. Student-driven book lists create a culture of personal voice. And this is especially important when building writers. Sometimes I have my students list what stands out to them in a novel they choose. For example, I had a student who read Jessi Kirby's *Moonglass*, a beautiful coming of age YA novel. In her list, my student referenced the ocean, sea glass, loss, determination, suicide, and mother—daughter dynamics as things that stood out for her in Jessi's book. At the same time, other students were reading the books they had selected and making their own specific lists. I had the students use these lists to generate a piece of their own writing that showcased their personal experience of any of the themes or elements they'd identified in their books.

When a young person reads and writes, they are actively building their own voice. When they learn what books they are drawn to, they have more agency in expanding that voice by identifying what drew them to a story in the first place. These are the kinds of rich connections that make reading special and ultimately lifelong.

As Grant Faulkner wrote... "a story, not its sprawl." I had... instead of the layers of a backstory, stuffing things in to fill the gaps." ...because each one must do so much... [I remind my] students that in all writing (not just with this form, but with all writing), a writer is always "noticing." We are noticing the specific senses that allow us to experience... sight, smell, taste, touch, sound... we are noticing the way people interact with each other, the way they speak (or don't); we are noticing all the small, bright, beautiful and interesting and heartbreaking. This noticing (and the specific choices we [make] because of it) allows us to create unique, vibrant worlds in small spaces, and these worlds begin at the sentence level.

The [logic] of the form is its attention to detail, a hint, instead of... each word in such a particular way... to create a full story. I like to tell a story through a [vignette] rather than...

Before starting th[is assignment], have your students practice noticing their worlds. Below, see the homework assignment I give my students. I share it with them as an online document. You could download it from the online resources. Over the years, many of my writing [teachers] have talked about... [how] writing is about "seeing"—about noticing... sight, smell, taste, touch, sound. For this assignment... and spend approximately thirty minutes noticing... what you see, smell, taste, touch... here, jot down notes about... to be complete sentences o[r a full vignette]... to try to record the unique... [one] reason I refer to these 100-word stories as "small,"... to detail, the prec[ise]... the introduction to th[is]... tell a b[ackstory]...

PART THREE

STRUCTURAL ELEMENTS

The Story and the Container

Structural elements provide the organization of the piece of writing. I tell my students that structure often begins with two things: the story they want to tell and making sure that story fits into the size of the container they have chosen. What's a container? The container is the form you're using for your story: a poem, or a 100-word story, or a 10,000-word short story, or a one-act play, or a novel. Each of these is a specific container.

17

PLOT AND ARC

Featured Authors: Jay Godwin, age 13, and Asma Almasy, age 17

REVIEW TERMS: sensory detail, character, setting

One of my graduate school mentors, the talented fiction writer Scott Nadelson, says that "Plot is just time: how writers manipulate time and move their characters through it" (2022). I love the succinctness of this definition. Could it be that simple? For me, it has always seemed one of the most challenging parts of writing. The plot. It's often what most people want to know when they hear about a book: What's it about? But maybe there aren't that many plots available to us as writers. After all, Joseph Campbell made a compelling argument for the prevalence of the hero's journey as an underlying western narrative structure (1949). And each culture has its own dominant plotlines. So, for the sake of simplicity in this chapter, we'll consider that plot is the series of events in a story and the specific choices a writer makes to organize and show these events.

When we write a story, we need to consider the following: given the world we've built and the characters we've created, does the order/crafting of events make sense? Are they plausible?

Let's read Jay Godwin's sweet story "Breaking Free."

Breaking Free

3 a.m. Under bright stars, I sat on the cold grass in a field near a local park with Alex, my best friend. We did this every night, eating cheddar Pringles® and talking about home, school, and the future.

But tonight was different.

He was the same, his dark blue hair falling across his pale forehead, his black eyes staring into my brown ones. Finally, he grabbed my hand. I heard his breath hitch. His hand was soft and warm. I smiled at him and squeezed back before we looked up at the sky. We wouldn't hide our feelings anymore.

—JAY GODWIN

DISCUSSION

1. What is the order of events in this story? How does Jay use time?

2. If plot is a series of events, what are the events that lead up to the end of this story?

3. How does Jay's integration of sensory detail, character, and setting help amplify this plot?

Of course, we can't talk about plot without talking about arc. Repeat after me: **a story has a beginning, middle, and end.** If it does not have a clear beginning, middle, and end, it is a vignette, and not a story.

And while we're on the subject of endings, it's important to remember that you don't have to like or agree with the ending, but it needs to be plausible. By plausible, I mean that the series of events leading to this ending make sense, given the context of the story. Too often, we accuse stories of having "bad" endings when the issue is that we wish they had ended differently. I encourage my students to think beyond our own interests, desires, experiences, and decide if the ending feels plausible.

One of the most important elements of a story arc is that the author is choosing this specific moment in time to tell the story for a reason. Often, this occurs when the main character (or characters) has a *moment of change or realization*. This shift is what moves the narrative from vignette into story arc. What is the realization for the character in teen author Asma Almasy's "Falling Apart"?

Falling Apart

After she fractured two ribs in a car crash, she began putting Band-Aids® where she felt the most broken.

Over her wrists, around her neck, on the fissure above her right eyebrow that threatened to split open when she had a migraine. No one saw them but her, the cracks in her skin tracing the pattern of her veins like shattered china carefully glued back together.

Afterwards, at the hospital, her battered reflection confronted her. She realized she could no longer trust her body to stay whole on its own.

Even so, bandages were not enough to keep her together.

—ASMA ALMASY

DISCUSSION

1. What is the order of events in this story? How does Asma use time?

2. Where is the clear beginning, middle, and end of the story?

3. Is the ending plausible? Satisfactory? Why/why not?

Writing Exercise

1. Have students choose from their portfolios one of the 100-word stories they have written so far.

2. What series of events do they use in this draft to lead up to the landing of their story?

3. Have them take notes on the story itself regarding other events that might make the story even more powerful, or create a more powerful, plausible ending.

Writing Practice

Have students revise their story with this new idea of arc in mind, using the notes they made during their exercise. Feel free to flip to the end of this book's revision section if you want tips to help students with revision, but for this practice, they should focus on how to strengthen their arc by crafting events that provide a clear beginning, middle, and end.

18

STRUCTURE AND FORM

Featured Author: Luca LaMarca, age 16

REVIEW TERMS: voice, setting

I often describe structure to my students as the purposeful organization of the big idea in a piece of writing. I have them ask themselves the following questions before they set out to write a piece:

How am I ordering things in this piece?

What is the flow of my ideas?

Where is it leading?

How am I using the form of this piece to showcase my ideas?

I show them examples of an interesting overall structure like Jason Reynold's *Long Way Down*, where the entire book takes place in a single-minute elevator ride. Or sometimes, books have internal structure (like this one, with chapters devoted to specific literary terms).

In Luca's 100-word story, he chose a unique setting and structure: this character's basement and the online Netflix® party event chat box the dialogue lives within.

Netflix Party Is Now Teleparty

Henry's computer screen shone coldly in his otherwise pitch-black basement. He adjusted his pillow, scrolling through Netflix's gritty, loveless recommendations. His phone buzzed.

 Wanna watch something else tonight? Kinda tired of godless monsters.

Henry frowned, sent back:

I've been excited for The Witcher® this whole day.

Kaylee countered:

 Apparently Bridgerton® is really good.

It's all frivolous ball gowns. Not my cup of tea.

 Let's just try it! You might enjoy some color.

Henry swallowed a spoonful of soggy cereal. Fine. He sent her the link.

Hours later, Henry had forgotten all about The Witcher.

 It's late

 But

 Another episode?

Absolutely.

—LUCA LAMARCA

It's important to consider the container that is holding a story. 100-word stories are one such container in that they have only 100 words, but this container is also about **shape**. The way the story appears on the page.

DISCUSSION

1. What about Luca's choices with structure make the story more interesting?

2. Why is the line "you might enjoy some color" so important, given the other details of the story? What does it say about these two characters' relationship?

3. What role does setting play in this story's structure?

Writing Exercise

Make a list of possible shapes that a 100-word story can have (all dialogue, all one paragraph, each line on its own, etc.).

Writing Practice

Choose one of the shapes from your list and write a 100-word story that focuses on using this shape to amplify the arc/content of the story.

19

GENRE

Featured Authors: Iris Vandevorst, age 15, and Gretchen McNeil

REVIEW TERMS: dialogue, specific detail

I t could be argued that authors need to know what genre they are writing before they set out to write the actual book. This is fair. Genre informs so much. But I waited to include it in this book until this section because people can be, well, *touchy* about genre.

I want to take a moment to discuss how certain genres sometimes get treated as if they aren't quality writing, especially in the older grades. I remember a teacher casually saying to me, "I just want them to read good writing and not that fantasy stuff." Um, there is some truly *excellent* writing in the fantasy genre. I feel like the notion of "good" books and "bad" books is an outdated concept (for more on this, see pages 77 and 112, my two essays in this book on building personal voice in reading and writing). I believe we need to look at the good work being done within each of the genres. The writing in fantasy, historical fiction, sci-fi, romance, etc. just keeps evolving mostly because people who write genre have a deep understanding of what it is their story is supposed to be doing *because* it is romance or fantasy or a speculative story.

Let's look at teen author Iris Vandevorst's fantasy story.

The Gatekeeper

"Hey, boy! I have the key, let me through!"

She shoves the filthy iron key into my face, the proof. I can just make out the numerous scars adorning her face in the candlelight.

Impatient, she swings the key back and forth on its weathered strip of twine.

She is the seventh, the final chosen one; once she enters the gate, my duty will be fulfilled.

I step aside, taking in the roughly hewn cave, the grand jade gate. My home, my tomb. I open the gate for the final time, watch her depart.

After centuries, the world finally fades.

—IRIS VANDEVORST

DISCUSSION

1. What elements give your students clues that this story is an example of the fantasy genre?

2. What specific details does Iris use to show these clues?

Horror and thrillers are two of those genres that make some English teachers turn up their noses (don't be too hard on yourself; we were all trained to do this!), but I have found horror and thrillers to be compelling and interesting ways to engage certain readers, especially those that innately crave being thrilled. John Ayto (1990) points out in the *Dictionary of Word Origins* that one of the original definitions of *thrill* is to "pierce with emotion" (529), and *horror* stems from the Latin for "hair standing on end, bristling" (286). Really, they both have to do with engaging that place in us that is curious about darkness and fear. A legit reason to read, in my opinion!

BuzzFeed® calls author Gretchen McNeil the "horror master" for good reason; she has an innate understanding of her genre. Let's read her story "Mirror, Mirror."

Mirror, Mirror

Jane didn't like the tarnished mirror in Grandmother's parlor. The girl it reflected didn't look like Jane. Dirty, emaciated, dressed in tatters.

"You're not me," Jane would say. "And I'm not you." She'd grin at the girl and primp her ringlets. The girl in the mirror would scowl.

"You're not me and I'm not you." Over and over. Smile, scowl.

Until one day when the girl smiled back.

"Why are you so happy?" Jane asked.

The girl reached through the mirror and gripped Jane's arm with icy fingers. "I'm not me and you're not you."

Then she sucked Jane through.

—GRETCHEN MCNEIL

DISCUSSION

1. What are some of the moments in Gretchen's story that create the thrill, that prickly moment when we feel afraid for this character?

2. How does she do that? What details does she use?

3. Have students make a list of genres. After, write their answers on the board and explore what tropes each of these traditionally

employ (I often have to write the definition of *trope* on the board for this assignment, so here is the one I use with my students: *common themes/devices/concepts used in writing*).

Writing Exercise

Have students look over their portfolios: What genres do they typically write in? Do they stick to one or branch out to different genres? What do they like about the genres they choose?

Writing Practice

Have students choose one of the genres they love and write a 100-word story that explores a common trope from this genre. Remind them that these stories still have all the elements of any fiction story (plus the added bonus of a genre!).

If you have time, a fun follow-up activity to this practice is to have students share their stories in pairs or groups, with a special introduction to the genre they chose and why they love it.

...icing." We are noticing the specific se... ...at in all writing (not ju... ...oticing the way people interact with each other, th... ...oticing all the small, bright specific things that mak... ...tbreaking. This noticing (and the specific choices we... ...brant worlds in small spaces, and these worlds begin... ...have your students practice noticing their worlds. ...y students. I share it with them as an online docu... ...from the online resources. Over the years, man... ...much of writing is about "seeing"—about noticin... ...smell, taste, touch, sound. For this assignm... ...approximately thirty minutes noticing e... ...bout what you see, smell, taste, touch... ..."vignette; they can be just words... ...you discover in that place, but al... ...reason I refer to these 100-v... ...rm is its attention to detai... ...the introduction to this... ...tell a story through a... ...gaps of text rather... ...rticular way beca...

...gic of the form is its a... As Grant Faulkner wrote i... ...f a story, not its sprawl. I hadn... instead of the layers of a backsto... stuffing things in to fill the gaps." An... way because each one must do so muc... ...dents that in all writing (not just with this... ...noticing." We are noticing the specific... ...are noticing the way people interact with eac... ...utiful and interesting and heartbreaking. This n... ...ecause of it) allows us to create unique, vibrant... ...s begin at the sentence level. Before starting th... ...m as an online document. You could do the s... ...sources. Over the years, many of my writ... ...ting is about "seeing"—about noticing t... ...r, smell, taste, touch, sound. For... ...and spend approximately thirty... ...here, jot down notes about... ...to be complete sentences o... ...to try to record the uniqu... ...ime just noticing—look... ...rd stories as "small... ...to detail, the prec... ...uction to th... ...tell a b...

...each one must do... a writer is always "noticin... ...h each other, the way they spea... ...teresting and heartbreaking. This no... ...aces, and these worlds begin at the se... ...ework assignment I give my students. ...ources o...

PART FOUR

REVISION

Intentional Feedback for Young Writers

My husband spent the first six years of his education career as a high school English teacher, and he often recalls a late-afternoon moment schlepping a sack full of essays to his car (back before Google Classroom and online drop boxes!) while watching a PE teacher walk unencumbered to his car with no bags at all. When his colleague saw my husband's load, he said, "We all make our choices, my friend." Fair enough.

So, for those of us who made this particular life choice (the one with the mounds of reading, assessing, and responding to written work), we can still lower some of the burden *and* make a meaningful impact. It is easy to get overwhelmed as an ELA teacher. In my credential program, a visiting high school teacher said that he knew he could snap his fingers and have close to two hundred writing samples in front of him just like that. So, before we snap, we should approach each writing sample intentionally.

One of my essential early teaching mentors, Marnie Masuda-Cleveland, who was (still is) an outstanding writing teacher, taught me that for each piece of writing we should intentionally give two pieces of meaningful praise and two pieces of meaningful feedback for growth. Matthew Johnson elaborates on this concept throughout his book *Flash Feedback* when he addresses targeted feedback (2020). This lets students know what to focus on in their writing and lets us, as teachers, know what to focus on while assessing the piece. Win-win.

Repeat after me: we are not their copyeditors.

Our primary role is to *develop* them as writers.

In his keynote at the 2017 Sierra Poetry Festival, Former California State Poet Laureate Dana Gioia references Robert Frost when he explores the idea of authentic writing as the practice of moving something from "delight to wisdom"—and that this practice takes time (2017). We must give our students the time and space to play with their writing, take risks, try things, and continue to shape and change their own work. We get hung up sometimes in education on data collecting and quantity and checklists rather than going more deeply into a single piece of writing to find and unlock its mysteries. This unlocking is the truest joy for me about writing, this movement from delight to wisdom, and I believe it is at the heart of growing a writer.

20

CHOICES, CHOICES— THE ART OF REVISION

Featured Authors: Charley Meyer, age 12, and Rachel Teferet

R evision is truly about the process of "re-seeing" your work for its innate potential. I like to refer to this process as "drafting" because I see it as a series of drafts of the story that we are trying to take from our imagination and apply to the page so a reader can ultimately engage with our vision.

Seventh grader Charley Meyer graciously agreed to let me share his drafting process for his 100-word story submission. When we first read Charley's story, we loved his vision but felt it could be amplified. Here was his first draft.

City of Crime (First Draft)

When he stepped outside his duplex, he was already filled with a sense of dread. Even on the city's quadricentennial, everywhere he looked was a crime scene waiting to happen: another robbery, another mugging, another gang ready to jump someone. He continued to walk, avoiding eye contact; the only thought in his mind was fleeing this wretched place, something he always wanted. But then he gazed at the neon signs, the starships above, and the smells of the vendor's foods. He felt a longing to stay, something he had never felt before. Perhaps there was something worthwhile here after all.

—CHARLEY MEYER

In this first draft, Charley showcased his vivid imagination; he already demonstrated skill at world-building and created a character who was clearly in crisis. We knew it was the start of something wonderful.

Kirsten, Beret, and I sent him the following notes for his first stab at revision:

Beret's suggestions:

Charley: I really like your idea of the main character reframing the way he sees his city. Up until this day, he has thought of it as a place to escape, but a certain special event helps him to see some potential in the city, some reasons to stay. Good stuff.

Perhaps you could start the piece slightly differently, to underline the character's "before thinking" and his "after thinking," and really emphasize the change of heart. Suggestion: "Every time he stepped outside his duplex, he was filled with a sense of dread. Everywhere he looked was a crime scene waiting to happen. . . ." But today was different.

I also think you might choose a different wording for the event happening that particular day, so the reader has something concrete in mind. I don't know what a quadricentennial entails, but I could easily conjure a mental picture for a parade, or a street fair, or a festival. Just a thought.

Kirsten's suggestions:

Charley: Your first sentence really draws the reader in! Is the conflict here that he does not want to stay anymore because of all of the crime, or is there something more at stake? Is there a person who might make him want to stay? I also loved how you withheld the futuristic details until towards the end. . . . Could you make the neon signs and vendor's foods also more futuristic? I think the last line is a little clichéd and obvious. Could he define why he had never felt a longing to stay before this moment? Or *how* do you think he will manage staying, what will need to change for him to make it work? I like the dread and heaviness of the place, and I also like the beauty that he finds.

Kim's suggestions:

Charley: I would love for you to play around with structure—with how this story looks on the page. Try putting some things on their own lines, try using white space. See what happens. If you don't like it, you can always go back to having it be one singular paragraph. Thanks, Charley!

Here is Charley's second draft.

City of Crime (Second Draft)

When he stepped outside his duplex, he was already filled with a sense of dread. Everywhere he looked was a crime scene waiting to happen. Just another robbery, another mugging, another gang poised to attack.

He continued to walk, avoiding eye contact; the only thought in his mind was fleeing this wretched place, something he had always wanted.

But today was different. It was the city's quadricentennial.

His senses were overcome by shiny neon signs, fantastic starships above, inviting smells of street vendors' food, and people dancing wildly. He felt a longing to stay, something he had never felt before.

—CHARLEY MEYER

Charley had already done so much good work in this on top of an already excellent first draft. But his editors still felt the story needed *something*. So, we followed up on one of Kirsten's suggestions: this character's motivation.

We asked him: What is at the heart of this story? What makes him feel all this?

Charley agreed to think about this. Then, he wrote us a late-night email where he explained he'd had a flash of inspiration. It was a dynamic solution: grief. This character had lost his mother. He revised again.

City of Crime (Third Draft)

When he stepped outside his duplex, he was already filled with dread. Everywhere he looked was a crime scene waiting to happen: another robbery, another mugging, another gang poised to attack.

He walked, avoiding eye contact; the only thought in his mind was fleeing this wretched place, something he had always wanted.

But today was different. It was the city's quadricentennial.

His senses were overcome by shiny neon signs, fantastic starships above, inviting smells of street vendors' food, and people dancing wildly. He felt a longing to stay, a feeling he hadn't felt since his mother's death.

—CHARLEY MEYER

Charley's idea to include the backstory with the mother made the story POP! Suddenly it had a backbone—a natural story arc. This character is grieving, and on this specific day something changes for him. As his editors, we pushed back just a bit more. Why would that make this quadricentennial meaningful for him? Why would it change things for him?

Here is the final revision of Charley's wonderful story.

City of Crime

He stepped outside his duplex, already filled with dread. Everywhere he looked was a crime scene waiting to happen: another robbery, another mugging, another gang poised to attack.

He walked, avoiding eye contact. The only thought in his mind was fleeing this wretched place, something he had always wanted.

But today was different. It was the city's quadricentennial. His mother had wanted to see this. His senses were overcome by shiny neon signs, fantastic starships above, inviting smells of street vendors' food, and people dancing wildly.

He felt something he hadn't felt since her death: a sudden longing to stay.

—CHARLEY MEYER

What an incredible evolution of this story—and it's also still very much the story it began as! We are very grateful to Charley for being willing to let us use this process for our chapter on revision. Often, writers only want the finished version of something in the world, but when Charley agreed to let us use each of his versions, we knew it would be useful for writers to see how ideas and discussion of all these elements we've been studying can allow a writer to re-see a story. The drafting process is a vibrant one, one in which a story gets to live a few different lives before settling into itself. And the result is a triumph.

I was telling one of my writer friends, Rachel Teferet, about this exciting experience with Charley, and she offered to show how a professional writer goes through this same process when revising a story with her own writing group. Here are her three versions of "Bantam Chicken," with notes from her wonderful writing peers: Liz Collins, Don Rodgers, and Heidi Lyss.

Bantam Chicken Version One (~180 Words)

I found what was left of Pell: a puddle of tawny feathers, a crumpled eggshell.

We had had that chicken since she hatched. Winter was late that year, so she lived in the living room in a cardboard box for one month.

The house smelled like poop. We never did that again.

Three years we had that intractable bird: she moved with us from ridge to ridge, saw all the roosters slaughtered, saw her brother's head get bitten off; she saw three generations of pullets, and she outlived all the first-year hens. She was picked on because she was small, and wild. We couldn't stop her from hopping the fence to forage, to horde piles of tiny eggs.

She died wild; maybe in the night, blind and squawking; or in the day, that sudden, painless death.

Maybe a raccoon, or, I hope, a coyote. It wasn't a hawk; hawks don't break eggs like that.

Outside the fence, in the kitkitdizze patch, her feathers breathe in the wind, and red ants carry away shards of her eggshell and congealed yolk.

—RACHEL TEFERET

Bantam Chicken Version Two, with Revision Notes (Exactly 100 Words)

I found what was left of Pell: a puddle of tawny feathers, crumpled eggshells. We'd had that chicken since she hatched. Winter was late that year, so she lived in the living room, the house stinking like poop.

For three years, Pell moved with us from ridge to ridge, saw three generations of pullets and all the roosters slaughtered. She was picked on because she was small and wild. We couldn't stop her from hopping the fence to horde her tiny eggs.

Now, red ants carry away shards, congealed yolk. In the kitkitdizze patch, her feathers breathe in the wind.

—RACHEL TEFERET

Editing notes from my critique group:

* In the first line, it's unclear if Pell was sitting on the eggs in her nest or being born from an egg herself!

* I also got feedback that folks couldn't picture a puddle of feathers, which helped reduce my word count in the third version.

* Another person thought that seeing her brother's head bitten off was more important than seeing three generations of pullets because it was more emotional and tied into the theme of mortality more closely.

Bantam Chicken Version Three (Exactly 100 Words)

I found what was left of Pell: tawny feathers, crumpled eggshells from children unborn. We'd had that chicken since she hatched. Winter was late that year, so she lived in our house, which stank like poop.

For three years, that intractable bird moved with us from ridge to ridge, saw a coyote decapitate her brother and three generations of roosters slaughtered. She was picked on because she was small and wild. We couldn't stop her from hopping the fence to horde her tiny eggs.

Now, red ants carry away congealed yolk. In the kitkitdizze patch, feathers breathe in the wind.

—RACHEL TEFERET

Sometimes it's hard to know where to start with revising. Often it just has to do with conversation about the piece, which is why creating a thriving writer's workshop in a classroom is so essential. However, we can also do this on our own as a writing exercise.

Writing Exercise

This is the "Revision Checklist" I use with any 100-word story my students decide to revise, as it can be a helpful jumping off place (Figure 20.1, also OR25). I tell them that if any of these isn't true, you need to work on that part of the story.

100-Word Story Revision Checklist

☐ My story has a clear, specific setting.

☐ My story has a clear POV. It is told in _____.

☐ My story has a distinctive main character, and this character is experiencing a moment of change.

☐ This character has a conflict. The conflict is _____.

☐ The story has a clear beginning, middle, and end. I use the structure to support this.

☐ I use sensory details to show this world. Two of my favorite examples are _____ _____.

☐ If I use dialogue, I use it to show character, enhance the story, or complicate the scene.

☐ My first line is the window into this story. My first line is _____.

☐ My last line creates a satisfying ending. My last line is _____.

☐ My story has a title. The title is _____.

Figure 20.1

21

TRY IT

Featured Author: Kim Culbertson

REVIEW TERMS: dialogue, setting, character

I n this chapter, students can practice revising a story they didn't write before writing and revising one of their own. Sometimes, it's less scary to pick apart someone else's work than to pick at your own. So let them pick me apart!

This is a story I wrote after helping clean out the band shed for my daughter's high school instrumental music program. The YA author in me just couldn't help but create two teen characters who were doing this activity together (with some backstory and subtext!).

When you have your students revise this, please let them know they can pick it apart, rearrange things, cut things, add things, etc. I'm not attached to this story and, honestly, will never know what they've done to it, so GO FOR IT!

Band Shed

"He said no sequins." She holds up a bedazzled vest, hopeful.

I pick through bags filled with mismatched plates, plastic forks, pink raffle tickets. "No costume vengeance."

"You're no fun." She drops the vest into a box oozing marching uniforms, ripped jazz shirts, two broken helmets, plumes removed.

She opens a cooler, emitting a sour-sweet smell. "Oh, gross. Nobody cleaned after the last comp. There's potato salad." She pauses. "Maybe I'll put it in his locker."

"Maybe you should see a therapist."

The fingers she uses to tuck her hair behind her ears visibly shake.

I cave. "Okay, the vest."

—KIM CULBERTSON

DISCUSSION

Some questions to consider before having students rewrite this story:

1. Who is the narrator? (What is the POV, but also *who* is this person specifically?)

2. Who else is in this scene? What has happened to her? What is at stake for her?

3. Identify places that could be more specific or clearer. What sensory details can be added or changed?

4. Where did you have questions? Can these questions be answered in a rewrite?

Writing Exercise
Have students look at these categories:

Genre	Action	Word
sci-fi	watching someone from a car	flower
romance	petting a dog	spoon
fantasy	stargazing	ordinary
detective	walking on a trail	blue
action/adventure	throwing a ball	problem

Figure 21.1

Here's an example story I wrote to show students how I chose one thing from each category and wrote a 100-word story incorporating each element. Below, I'm providing the revisions I did over a 30-minute period, with ten minutes devoted to each draft.

genre: detective

action: watching someone from a car

word: spoon

Early Draft: "Spoon Trouble" (70 words)

He was so tired of dead bodies, of watching people from cars, of all of it. How many times had he sat here in this seat, trying to eat ramen with a spoon? Why did Klara insist on always getting him a spoon? He missed Rachel. She never asked a spoon to do a fork's job.

"Ready?" Klara leaned into his open window. "They're ready for us." He wasn't ready.

—KIM CULBERTSON

After reading my first draft, I decided that I needed to name the character. It would help me see him better if I gave him a specific name. I also realized a sense of place was lacking, and so I added some world details. Finally, the character needed a reason to be struggling with this moment in his professional life—so I gave him Rachel (a former partner he'd lost in the line of duty) and this backstory allowed me to explore that theme of loss.

Second Draft: "Ready" (95 words)

Kevin was so tired of dead bodies, of watching criminals from cars. How many times had he sat here in this seat, trying to eat ramen with a spoon? Why did Klara always insist on getting him a spoon? He missed Rachel. Even after ten years. She never asked a spoon to do a fork's job.

Outside, the lights of the city spangled the puddled road. He wished it would rain for more than a half hour at a time. "Ready?" Klara leaned into his open window.

He wondered if he'd ever be ready again.

—KIM CULBERTSON

I liked some of the structural changes I made in this draft (I especially liked where I landed the last line). And I tried to amplify the theme of loss through the weather by having him miss the way it used to rain. Thematically, I knew he was struggling not just with the loss of his former partner but also with time passing in general.

For my final draft, I knew I would mostly be tinkering with language (to add those five words I needed) and to look closely at my sentences to make sure this world was as specific as possible.

Final Draft: "Dead Tired" (100 words)

Kevin was tired of dead bodies, of watching criminals from cars. How many times had he sat here, trying to eat ramen with a spoon? Why did Klara always insist on spoons? He missed Rachel. Even after ten years. She never asked a spoon to do a fork's job.

Klara rapped on the edge of his open window. "They're ready for us." Outside the lights of the city spangled the puddled road. He wished it would rain more than twenty minutes at a time. Didn't it used to rain for days? "Ready?"

He wondered if he'd ever be ready again.

—KIM CULBERTSON

For this exercise, use the thirty minute, three-draft approach, with ten minutes devoted to each draft. Have students write their own 100-word story based on the options from Figure 21.1 (page 108), and then consider the following questions as they revise it. Remind them that revision means to *re-see*—to *look again* at what they've written.

DISCUSSION

You can do this in pairs, individually, or as a class, but as students look at their work on the page, ask:

1. What is my story about? What's the conflict, the problem for my characters?

2. What are the obstacles keeping these characters from what they want?

3. Where is the story set? How does place inform the story?

4. Instead of looking at what's there, take a moment to consider what is *not* currently on the page. What can I add or develop or enhance to amplify my story?

5. Revision is a conversation—with the writer, with the editor, with the characters. What questions can we ask the story to make it richer, deeper, more engaging?

Writing Practice

Have students choose a story from their portfolios and answer the above questions for their selected story. Have them turn in both the original draft and the revised version of their story.

Creating a Culture of Personal Voice in Readers and Writers: Part Two

Once, at a doctor's appointment with my teenage daughter, the woman checking us in saw my daughter's bag from the bookstore where she worked in high school. "Oh!" she exclaimed (as if seeing a giraffe in the window). "How wonderful. Does anyone read anymore?" You'd be surprised how often I get a version of this when people hear I have devoted my life to various versions of reading.

Rather than finding a corner in which to huddle in despair, I like to pose this question to my students on a fairly regular basis:

Why *do* we read?

Often, ideas emerge that we read to understand and make sense of a bigger world and connect with another person's interior world. Ultimately, as the character of C. S. Lewis said in the film *Shadowlands*, we read to know we're not alone. To take this idea a step further in this book, I want to pose this question:

Why, as teachers, do we often get hung up on regulating the content—the specific texts that let our students do this?

If the true goal is to get them to analyze, find patterns, seek out relationships, study plot, understand language and literary devices, why must that be through *The Great Gatsby*? (Which is a book I adore, by the way.) But why must it always be the same books for a classroom? Don't get me wrong, I think there is value in whole-classroom reads; they allow everyone to be a part of a larger conversation. My daughter's middle school teacher used to start the year with a class read. Then, after that, she organized student-driven lit circles where students chose the books they wanted to read and discussed them in small groups using a system of analysis she had developed with them during that first class read.

We must all look at the way we create a culture that values personal choice in our classrooms, that values and promotes personal instinct when it comes to reading. Then, let's teach students how to talk about their choices. This process is part of building not just a reader, but also a writer. We can't do this if our students feel their choices and instincts aren't valued, that the only language and story and writing in the room is from a certain book that a teacher has deemed school worthy. However, I know that sometimes we don't have the sort of broad selections of books we wished we had in our rooms, which is one reason to love 100-word stories even more. They provide this selection of easily accessible stories so that students can connect with voices outside of their own.

I have written five young adult novels. In each of my books, I strive to create an authentic voice. I'm able to do this because I had teachers who taught me my voice mattered, that my instincts were strong, that what I valued was worth valuing. Still, even now, as an adult published author, I am vulnerable to bias and judgment; there are people who devalue my work in blatant or subtle ways, who tell me my books are "fluffy" or "light" or—perhaps my least favorite—"for girls" (because they have a female main character. Incidentally, no one ever says *The Catcher in the Rye* is "for boys," but, again, that's another essay as well). Still, I am lucky because I feel strongly enough about my personal voice not to listen to (most of) them.

It's subtle, this valuing, this encouraging of students to identify what they want to read as a way of strengthening their own voices. And sometimes it's challenging when they might not like the books we value. Sometimes it's hard to put our egos aside. Sometimes it's hard to hear their choices without judgment and without assuming our book list should be everyone's book list. Our goal with everything we do in school is to teach them to do this on their own someday—to inquire, to make connections, to see a world outside of themselves. We are in the business of building readers and writers and thinkers. Armed with a clear sense of voice and values, students have a powerful ally when they approach their education. Human curiosity has a wonderful habit of winning. That boy I mentioned earlier in Part One of this essay, the one who claimed he wasn't a reader, ended up connecting with *Brave New World* and creating a personal project that studied the evolution of the dystopian writers who paved the way for his beloved sci-fi series.

Most importantly, let's not be the ones who tell them that what they are drawn to doesn't matter. Instead, let's guide them to texts that will illuminate their futures and help establish their young voices, and then let's give them the tools to talk about why. When we value what students care about, we tell them "I value *you*: I value your instincts, your interests, your perspective." And I believe this valuing can lead not just to a lifelong love of reading, but also to a lifelong active *seeking* to find connections and a place in the world.

This foundation helps build them as writers. At the 2017 Sierra Poetry Festival, Dana Gioia said that "Poetry originates in a particular place, in a particular time, in an individual body" (2017). I think this is true for any act of writing or, perhaps in a bigger sense, any act where we're asked to create something out of nothing—which is what writing is. It's why it's scary for so many of our students. This is why we give them templates and forms and structure, like the 100-word stories in this book. We're scaffolding. But what I think we forget to give them sometimes is the reminder that they have access to a specific, individual place and a specific, individual self *right now, immediately*, and it's this access, this delving into the individual place and self and experiences, that provides a treasure trove of authentic writing tools.

The driving question of the moment, then, is how do we balance allowing our students to find their specific voices while still creating a synthesized writing community in our classrooms? I believe developing a community of writers based on valuing unique voice strengthens a classroom. Teaching students that their differences are powerful and that they must support each other within this community only elevates that power. We show them that each of their voices is irreplaceable— they can't be replicated and can't be compared to the writer sitting next to them. The power of the collective is strong when each individual voice is valued.

22

PHOTO PROMPTS

Featured Authors: Estlin Miller, age 17, and Kristin Dwyer and Misa Sugiura

REVIEW TERMS: POV, character, setting

I love writing prompts. I start each creative writing class with a prompt that the students work on for fifteen minutes. Sometimes I give them a poem and have them choose a line from it as a jumping off place for a story or poem; sometimes I give them a group of words they must use in a scene; sometimes I give them a photo prompt.

In one of my 100-word story Zoom® workshops, I gave the following photo as a prompt (Figure 22.1).

Figure 22.1

One of the writers in my workshop, Estlin Miller, wrote this story:

Waiting

Fractured sunlight trickles in like raindrops through the high arched station ceiling. Mark watches the four o'clock train pull in, smug steam curling over the floor. Each face passes, unremarkable, like blurred buildings on a long drive.

Maybe she forgot that he was waiting for her here. He used to love being the one to remind her of things like this.

The doors shut with a loud *kathunk* that startles him. More steam rolls weakly across his shoes, and a gray cloud passes outside the skylights as he turns the ring in his pocket.

She didn't forget. Not this time.

—ESTLIN MILLER

DISCUSSION

1. How does the author use the setting and imagery to create tension in the story?

2. Choose two lines from the story that stood out to you. Why?

3. Remember, what elevates something from a vignette to a story is the way an author creates a moment of change or realization for a character so that the landing feels satisfying for the reader. What moment of change or realization happens for the character in this story?

Two professional YA authors I adore also graciously agreed to write to this photo prompt and I'm happy to share that they both had completely different takes on it (which is the beauty of photo prompts). Here are Kristin's and Misa's stories.

The Ticket

He buys a ticket every time and waits.

He watches people exiting in a hurry, or ones leaving slowly as they stare up at the ceiling in awe. He thinks there's something telling about how a person gets off a train and he wonders what kind of person he might be if he finally uses his ticket.

He loves this place between beginnings and endings. Everyone is on their way. No one has arrived, yet.

He buys a ticket every time. His fingers wrap around the paper, ready to stand, before he remembers.

There isn't anywhere to go.

She's gone.

—KRISTIN DWYER

Quitter

We sped through entire cities. Past lonely fields, along windswept lakeshores, under looming mountains. Life inside the train was tedious and grim, and I longed to get off, but a mellifluous voice described constantly the wonders we would encounter at our destination. Golden towers! An abundance of riches and creature comforts! All we could ever want—if we simply stayed on the train. So I did, until one day I didn't.

"What if you never make it there?" everyone asked.

I watched as they pulled away into the light. Then I walked out of the station and into the world.

—MISA SUGIURA

Writing Exercise

When my students write to photo prompts, I like to remind them to think about the following things before writing. Use these questions as a pre-writing exercise for the photo:

1. You have a clear setting (it's a photo), but why is this setting essential to the arc of your story?

2. Who is this character within this world? What do they want? What's at stake for this character?

3. What is important about this one place in time? What about the story needs telling *right now*?

4. How can you create a moment of change or realization for your character in this story?

Writing Practice

Now that they've answered these, have them write a 100-word story based on the photo (see Figure 22.1). When they finish, break them into small groups or pairs, and have them share their stories. Have them record the different ways each writer responded to the photo:

- What were the similarities in the stories?

- What were the differences?

- What specifics made each story unique?

This can also lead into a discussion of why our own point of view is special as writers. Even with the exact same prompt, we all come up with different images, characters, and conflicts. Three cheers for imagination!

One More Fun Photo Prompt Idea: **Photo Flash**

I love doing a "photo flash" with my students. I show them three photos, **one at a time**. First photo, they do a three-minute writing sprint. Second photo, three-minute writing sprint. Third photo, three-minute writing sprint. No intros, no suggestions, just tell them to write whatever comes to their minds for each of these three photos.

Next, I have them go back through their writing and find the "connective tissue." Where do they see links between their writings? Taking this link (whether it is thematic or character-driven or setting-based), I have them do a five-minute writing sprint to create a 100-word story, using the connective inspiration they discovered.

23

CHOOSING A TITLE

Featured Author: Brinda Ambal, age 16

REVIEW TERMS: structure/form

A title can do some heavy lifting for this small, bright form of 100-word stories, especially since it's not included in the word count! It can provide metaphorical, symbolic, or thematic guidance. It can give a sense of tone for the story. It can even help kick off the voice the author is hoping to showcase in the piece.

Have students read the following two drafts of teen author Brinda's story, exploring how when her title changes, so does her story:

Ten Times

One two three four five six seven eight nine ten.

If only I could write that ten times because I write this at one in the morning, with no strength left in my two leaden arms. I write this after a three-mile run and a four-minute shower, after sitting through five hours of Zoom and taking six pages of hand-cramping notes. After preparing seven slides for my club meeting, sewing eight masks, and answering nine emails,

I'm

still

writing–

I need to work ten times harder tonight before I can slip into sleep and work ten times harder again tomorrow.

—BRINDA AMBAL

As editors, we loved what Brinda was doing with the structure in this story—the rhythmic use of counting to ten to demonstrate that intense push so many students feel in their teenage years around their schedules and obligations. However, we felt she could try to amplify those same qualities through a change of title and a more vibrant ending. After a conversation with Brinda, she came back with this revision.

Multiples of Ten

One two three four five six seven eight nine ten.

I write this down at one in the morning, with no strength left in my two leaden arms. I write this after a three-mile run and a four-minute shower, after sitting through five hours of Zoom, and taking six pages of painstaking, hand-cramping notes. I write it after preparing seven slides for my club meeting, sewing eight masks, and answering nine emails.

I'm

still

writing–

Because I need to work ten times harder tonight before I can slip into sleep. My life is relentless multiples of tens. Again and again.

—BRINDA AMBAL

DISCUSSION

How does her new title do more work for the story than the original one?

Writing Exercise

Have your students look through their portfolios at the 100-word stories they've written in class so far. Have them check their titles. Are the titles doing as much work as they should be?

Writing Practice

Have your students write a fresh 100-word story where they focus on choosing a title first and then writing the story to fit it. After, explore with them how this is different from writing the story first.

24

ANNOTATING A STORY USING WHAT YOU'VE LEARNED

Featured Author: Lachlan Ryan, age 16

REVIEW TERMS: all of them

Now it's time to put it all together. The following handout, "Terms for Annotating a Story" (Figure 24.1, or OR29), can work for any 100-word story your students study, including the ones they write.

Annotation simply means "taking notes" on a specific text. It's using knowledge to analyze a piece of writing. It's best if students can have a paper copy of the text in front of them so they can scribble all over it. I sometimes even do annotation gallery walks where students can walk around and see the notes other students have made on their handouts.

Terms for Annotating a Story

Read teen author Lachlan Ryan's wonderfully rich story "Green Land" and annotate it to delve into how he uses all the devices we've been studying.

The following terms are useful for your notes:

point of view	"the stakes"	active language
character	theme	dialogue
setting	sensory, specific detail	first/last line
voice/tone	imagery	subtext/backstory
conflict/tension	symbolism	plot
arc	structure/form	genre

And don't forget to look at the role the title plays!

Green Land

Down a road paved mostly by potholes, across a beach more stones than sand, I used to scramble along a salt whitened tree to a secret green clearing. Shrouded in the smell of the sea, we cousins alone knew this place, hidden below our grandparents' house.

It used to be a place where clothes could be snagged, torn, where neat hair could be mussed, where we promised to never share it with the adults.

It was ours.

But now I stand by the cracked tree, in the overgrown grass, and I'm showing you. Now I'm breaking promises.

Now it's yours.

—LACHLAN RYAN

Figure 24.1

25

OTHER COOL STUFF

The 100-word story form can work for many other kinds of writing. You can have your students write 100-word essays, 100-word memoirs, 100-word poems, 100-word film reviews, 100-word screenplays, and more. I remind them that the emphasis on form and word count is an intentional, purposeful kind of focus on their sentences that can make their overall writing stronger.

One of the ways I use this form in my English 11/12 Composition class is to have my students write a 100-word descriptive essay. For this assignment, they choose a specific object and then describe it in detail. I remind them that this is a special kind of form because it forces them to make specific, creative choices to meet the word count.

I tell my students they can play around with structure, but this essay does need to be exactly 100 words (not including the title, of course) and have a clear beginning, middle, and end. The emphasis for this essay is mostly atmospheric (meaning it creates a *mood*) and should focus on using creative language to craft a detailed and engaging sensory description of this object and its role in the world.

I also ask them to use the object as the title of the essay and encourage them not to mention it in the actual essay, but that is entirely up to you. My students are used to me giving them a lot of parameters.

Also, I tend to do this assignment in October, hence my example essay.

Jack-O'-Lantern

Along the streets, each bright, orange orb glows in the gloaming. Some rest on porch steps, some in dark windows, and some line the edges of yards. One is cut in the face of a screeching demon, one with a crooked smile, and another in the jagged pattern of a tree. Each one, unique.

As night falls, their glow casts a yellowed, flickering light throughout the neighborhood.

Halloween night, the shouts of children surround them; the sound of doors opening and shutting, the cry of "trick or treat!" fills the air.

The pumpkins sit sentinel, marking another October, almost gone.

—KIM CULBERTSON

If you are working on personal narrative in your class, you can also have your students write a 100-word memoir. This is especially helpful as a lead-up to writing longer narrative pieces or personal statements for college essays, or even just fun little pieces for back-to-school night to put on each student's desk for their grown-ups to read. The award-winning author and writing teacher Sands Hall crafted this 100-word memoir as an example.

Setting the Table

Fork on the left. Spoon on the right. Mom puts her hand over mine and turns the knife so the sharp edge faces in.

"In the olden days," she says, "if the blade faced out, the person sitting on that side could think you meant him harm."

Suddenly I'm in a cave. A sheep roasts in the fireplace. Men wear kilts, and sit at long tables.

One of them stares, gasps, stands. He draws his knife.

No! says the man beside him. I didn't mean—

"So we place it facing in," Mom says. "Think of it as knife kissing plate."

—SANDS HALL

Another fun activity is to have students write 100-word scripts. Here's a beautiful short film script called "The Believer" by Gary Wright, an award-winning actor, screenwriter, and playwright, which shifts the need for belief to an atypical place in this little family:

The Believer

FADE IN:

INT. JUSTIN'S BEDROOM - NIGHT

JUSTIN (8) sound asleep. His door creaks open . . .

MOM (30s) tiptoes in, slips a hand under his pillow, pulls out a BABY TOOTH.

    JUSTIN

Ummm? I thought Daddy was the tooth fairy?

    MOM

    (surprised)

Oh . . . Did you catch him, too?

JUSTIN
(nods)
I didn't want to wreck it for him, so I played like I was asleep.
MOM
Good thinking.
She touches his forehead, steps out into the—
HALLWAY
DAD (30s) is waiting.
DAD
How'd it go?
MOM
Perfect.
DAD
He still believes?
MOM
(smiles)
Yes.
(touches his cheek)
He still believes.
FADE OUT

—GARY WRIGHT

The possibilities with this form are truly endless. It's one of the reasons I've fallen in love with it over the years. Recently, a student who was new to the form told me after class, "I thought it was going to be easy. It's *not* easy." It's not easy because it requires such close attention to every single word. The form's container, its boundaries to push against, help fine-tune a writer's initial vision and stretch those revision muscles. This practice can then translate to longer work.

Most importantly, I try not to fall into the quantity/quality trap. In all honesty, most of the longer assignments I give are just not as good as the shorter ones, not as focused, not as revised, because they are busy kids, and shorter assignments give us all more time to work closely and purposefully on a piece of writing. We have more time to walk around in the sentences. One of my former colleagues (who asked to remain anonymous for this book) told me that she once assigned a ten-page paper and the majority were *terrible*. She sticks to three-to-five pages now (tops). I tend to stick to two-to-three. Good writing takes time, precision, and a close study of both the macro and micro elements of a work's overall purpose. These small, bright things let us do this over and over with our students in easily digestible packages. They have revolutionized the way I teach, and I am so grateful for the opportunity to share them with you in this book.

Works Cited

Andrade, Jorge Carrera. [1940] 2011. "Origin and Future of the Microgram." In *Micrograms*. Translated from the Spanish by Alejandro de Acosta and Joshua Beckman. Seattle, WA: Wave Books.

Ayto, John. 1990. *Dictionary of Word Origins*. New York: Arcade Publishing.

Campbell, Joseph. 1949. *The Hero with a Thousand Faces*. Bollingen Foundation: Princeton, NJ: Princeton University Press.

Canin, Ethan. 2009. In-person interview with Kim Culbertson. October 10. Wordslingers Festival. The Center for the Arts. Grass Valley, CA.

Cartan, Michael. 2007. Personal conversation.

Chandler, Raymond. 1950. "The Simple Art of Murder." *Saturday Review of Literature*, April 15: 13–14.

Fitzgerald, F. Scott. 1936. "The Crack-Up." *Esquire*. February 1: 41.

Frost, Robert. 1939. *Collected Poems of Robert Frost*. New York: Halcyon House.

Gioia, Dana. 2017. Keynote Speaker. Sierra Poetry Festival. Nevada County, CA: April 1. https://www.youtube.com/watch?v=tQSPRhjnacw.

Haig, Matt. 2018. "Books Save Lives." *Waterstones Blog*. May 11.

Hall, Sands. 2008. Private Fiction Workshop. Spring.

Johnson, Matthew. 2020. *Flash Feedback: Responding to Student Writing Better and Faster— Without Burning Out*. Thousand Oaks, CA: Corwin.

Nadelson, Scott. 2022. Personal conversation. September 28.

Reynolds, Jason. 2017. *Long Way Down*. New York: Atheneum.